IMPROVING COMPLEX ORGANIZATIONS

All rights reserved. No part of this book may be reproduced or transmitted in any form or by any means, electronic or mechanical, including photocopying, recording, or by an information storage and retrieval system-- without permission in writing from the publisher.

Copyright 2016
Produced in the United States of America.
Briggs, J. Paul

Includes bibliographical references

Dedicated to all those striving to improve cost-effectiveness, particularly in government organizations and large scale businesses.

Table of Contents

Prologue..5

1. **Goals**: *Progressing Toward TOP Success*...............7

2. **Cost-Effectiveness**: *Making an IMPACT*..........33

3. **Process Review**: *Establishing Continuous Reform*..73

4. **Top Management**: *Making a Positive Difference*..93

5. **Managers**: *Bringing Out the Best*.....................121

6. **Employees**: *Being the Best*................................165

7. **Controls**: *Improving Performance and Accountability*..195

8. **Change**: *Reorganizing with Purpose*................253

9. **Structure**: *Optimizing by Standardizing*.........271

10. **Functions**: *Ensuring Success of Critical Operations*..291

Bibliography..361

Prologue

Complex organizations are any large scale organizations of the private, public, or non-profit sectors that provide operational, administrative, and executive direction; possess at least three hierarchical levels of management; maintain formal as well as informal rules for organizing; and coordinate multi-purposed tasks for the meeting of goals. There are many sizes, shapes and purposes of complex organizations but due to operational necessity and bureaucratic tendency, all face common challenges. This book serves as an aid in identifying and responding effectively to the many challenges of government or big business.

Organizational leaders know the way to success is through constant improvement and adaptation to environmental change, manager/employee attrition, and the need for technological improvement. This book offers a practical guide by suggesting the top ten things to consider in each chapter or subject area in order to improve complex organizations.

Anyone working in an office environment can find humor in the cynical but sadly realistic comic-strip "Dilbert," in which a small group of employees struggle to make sense of an all-too-typical insane work environment. Alternatively, this book is intended to give those striving to improve the office situation and the overall complex organization many suggestions toward actually making a real difference. Despite all the stigmatization and burdens of bureaucracy, complex organizations can be reformed into successful performers.

This book addresses the most pressing issues confronting complex organizations and serves as a reference guide for executives, managers, employees and consultants on a broad range of management, operational and administrative areas. In particular, the *"Ten Organizational Priorities (TOP) Model"* is developed to display the steps needed to assess and improve complex organizations. The *"Integrated Management, Planning, Assessment, Correction and Tracking (IMPACT) Model"* is developed to show how organizational structures can be designed for continuous improvement. These two models together can generate a "TOP IMPACT" in the improvement of cost-effectiveness and organizational success.

Chapter 1

Goals: Progressing Toward TOP Success

In their study of complex organizations, organizational theorists have long attempted to learn what makes organizations successful or unsuccessful, highly functional or dysfunctional. Bowman and Deal[1] note that there have been four basic ways that individuals have approached the study of complex organizations:

For *"rational"* theorists, the focus is on determining the extent to which the organization sets detailed production goals and develops the most efficient structures and production lines for achieving these goals.

For *"human resource"* theorists, the focus is on how well the organization focuses on the needs, skills, and values of employees and tailors the work to meet these needs.

For *"political"* theorists, the focus of study is on the process and outcome of internal and external struggles for power, resources, personnel, and status. The individuals and organizations that are most adept at

---

[1] L. Bowman and T. Deal. *Reframing Organizations*. San Francisco: Jossey-Bass, 1997.

"jungle warfare," or basically doing anything that might be needed to get ahead, will be most successful.

For *"symbolic"* theorists, the focus is on the "underlying meaning" behind organizational perceptions, behavior, and performance as it can be a hidden harbinger for accurately forecasting potential and success. For example, employees' disgruntled attitudes, misconduct, and poor performance is often linked to managers' pursuit of the rational or political approaches. There might also be the hypocritical concern for how the organization is portrayed to the customer rather than any real desire to actually fulfill agency mission or stated purposes.

Each approach is useful for analyzing organizational behavior. The problem is that an organization has so many moving parts that a more holistic theory is needed to help to understand what makes an organization successful. There are instruments to measure general social climate, management styles, types of decision making, and management-employee personality styles, but these only tell part of the story, only give one a sense about what might be working well or ailing an organization. To produce successful organizations, it is not enough to know that management styles or personalities match, or decision making is too authoritarian, or the communication of goals and purpose between hierarchal levels is incongruent. What is needed is the ability to define the essential leadership, process, management and outcomes that make for a successful organization, and how all parts of an organizations work for the good of the whole.

This is achieved by turning to an *"open systems"* approach, where the interdependency of parts becomes the focus. Here, leadership, structure, goals, are interdependent with products, people, and services, and work together to accomplish the missions of the organization, as managers operate with clear goals and behave in an accountable and effective manner.

Ten Organizational Priorities (TOP) Model

The ten most important organizational priorities, goals and attributes of successful organizations are:

1. Quality Leadership
2. Unified Purpose and Plan
3. Unified Command
4. Unified Effort and Culture
5. Minimal Organizational Structure
6. Simplified Workflow Process
7. Built-in Accountability
8. Technical Proficiency
9. Quality Input and Output
10. Effective Communication

To organize, lead, evaluate, and improve government and big businesses, the focus must be on these parts and on the awareness of the relationships between parts. Each step of the model (1-10) is placed in rank order of importance, and each has a cause-effect relation on subsequent steps. Top leadership must apply a simultaneous approach to advance development for the future while improving the present to achieve continuously improvement. A brief description of each priority for organizational success is described below, followed by a theory on how TOP Model can be used to improve cost-effectiveness of any organization, however complex it may be.

1. Quality Leadership

Quality leaders attract, recruit and develop quality senior managers and middle managers; it is their number one priority. Quality leaders find and position managers who are leaders with the proper skills and expertise, and the appropriate personality and temperament to best get the job done and succeed long into the future. These leaders succeed just as the top manager does, by attracting the best quality candidates for jobs and then nurturing and expanding the strengths of all employees.

Leadership is embodied in managers who know what leading means, and show the way in their attitudes and actions, always finding ways to make contributions for the organization, and benefit employees in the process. Quality employees seek leadership roles by offering meaningful ideas for organizational improvement. Quality leaders know how to develop good ideas and the people so that the ideas keep flowing and the employees keep generating them and being properly rewarded for them.

There is a big difference between managers who lead versus those who manage to survive. "Managers who lead" have vision, a balanced common-sense approach, a clear idea of what actions would make a significant contribution, and through their daily operational choices, such as staff assignment and direction, provide a firm understanding of what would work best toward attaining organizational long term goals and short term objectives.

Managers who lead communicate effectively to others on the meaningfulness of the work being done and its worth. Their employees believe that their contribution is vital to the success of the organization; that their efforts are having an impact. They appropriately match tasks with individual knowledge, skills, abilities, and interests and are able to select appropriate people to perform group tasks effectively. Leaders understand employees' strengths and weaknesses, as well as their background, experience, and personality, and instinctively know how to mix and match each for the best tactical results.

Leaders know how to balance staff and organizational needs. They show sufficient patience in disciplining, but are quick to correct, and know when and how to train, retrain, hire, fire, and reposition staff. They keep their employees gainfully engaged and balance the workload equitably, keeping the organizational dynamic moving at a high achievement level with employees enjoying their work and feeling fully involved, fulfilled, and energized by it.

Leaders keep well informed and are accessible to all employees, open to their thoughts on how to improve the organization, always grateful for such input and encouraging of all to continue to bring their ideas forward. They are keenly analytical and discern when information is useful and how it can be used, or what additional information might be needed.

Leaders do not need the credit for doing well. They share the credit, generously giving others their due. The intentional and selfish denial of credit to others for ones' own advantage disqualifies the individual as a leader. Leaders do not show undue favor toward individuals for reasons other than the good of the organization, and have no time to hold idle chit-chats with friendly staff. Leaders have little or no time for any idle discussion for their energy is channeled into moving the organization forward. Happy and healthy relations are a natural byproduct of hard work and success by all.

Managers who lead know how to motivate and guide all types of people. Not all managers are born leaders, but they can learn to be so by relying on a basic sense of fairness and propriety, and by "putting oneself into others' shoes." Considering organizational needs and employee needs, the manager must know both how to work well with employees who are highly motivated and need little guidance as well as with those who work well only if closely supervised and highly structured. Leaders know what work can be done by whom and assign tasks and nurture people to bring the best out of all their employees.

Quality managers do not hold meetings without a worthwhile purpose, and only include those who need to be included in meetings, not wasting the time of others unnecessarily. Senior leaders do hold structured meetings within a regular schedule to keep other managers and team leaders informed, to gain feedback on the status of their activities, and to maintain effective vertical and horizontal accountability of all to one another. They also hold periodic meetings with all employees to inform them directly on organizational activities and accomplishments, to correct long term and immediate direction and encourage continued high performance toward defined goals, to ask for ideas about improvements, to ask for management feedback and status reports, and to appropriately acknowledge those who deserve special credit for recent accomplishments.

Quality leaders embody the meaning of integrity, treating people fairly and adhering to the highest level of ethical principle and practice. Most managers have more problems with the sin of omission than commission when it comes to integrity. Often when one's own advancement or survival hinges on staying silent, managers easily rationalize the wrong of doing nothing, allowing one's peers or authorities to proceed unjustly without reproach undermining the stability, morale, and trust of employees. Leaders always do what is right and just in a forthright manner, protecting their staff and others from undue abuse or injustice.

2. Unified Purpose and Plan

Planning is orchestrated by management to achieve organizational goals and objectives. Ineffective organizations use planning as an academic or paperwork exercise to fulfill some requirement often set by higher authorities outside the organization. These efforts are simply a waste of time and energy.

Planning should be measured by the time spent against outcomes realized. With the proper attitude and planning concepts clearly understood, planning promotes success.

The three plans that need to be unified in order for planning and implementation to succeed are:

- Strategic Plans;
- Performance Plans; and,
- Project Plans.

Managers attempting to develop unified plans begin with an organization's stated or statutory mission or major long range business goals. The "*strategic plan*" sets broad goals in measurable terms that tie to the missions and long range business goals. The "*performance plan*" sets specific operationally defined objectives and tasks that address strategic goals within ones available resources. The "*project plan*" is the manager's plan for implementation, stated as efficiently as possible the manner in which the Performance Plan objectives will be met, within what timeframes, and detailing who is going to do what.

The planning process needs to bring together the best ideas within the organization. This involves seeking input from employees at all levels or involving a representative span of employees. The greater is the input, the more fruitful will be the planning and greater will be the organizational commitment. Planning is only useful to the extent that it pays off by directing organizational energy and advancing organizational purpose.

3. *Unified Command*

A unified command means that everyone in the organization is aware of who is in charge and respects their leader(s). A unified command does not imply a hierarchical chain of command within a centralized organizational structure; it can be a very informal structure. It is simply the commitment to the authority vested in the positions at the various management levels, and to the plans and goals of its leaders at every level. This commitment is demonstrated by the attitude of supervisors and employees, the sustaining of open communication within and among organizational levels, the fair balance of employee workload, and the consistency and effectiveness of work effort.

When there is unified command, managers and employees bring a sense of team effort in achieving work goals, and do not mind lending a hand to help other teams accomplish their objectives if needed. Within a unified command there is respect both within ones' own ranks but also for others' supervisors and employees, as it is the organization that counts. This respect does not mean being blind or silent about each others' shortcomings, but it is an environment where one can admit ones' own errors or failings and where others will tolerate them provided corrective actions are taken reasonably swiftly.

A unified command is stymied when managers attempt to exhibit control through fear, defensiveness, turf-control, self-interest, and empire building. In such environments, supervisors close-off communications, choosing to limit discussion with their first line superior and rarely ever speak to or hear from their second line superior. The lack of unified command means supervisors rarely include employees in decision making and there is no open door policy seeking employee input. Instead, supervisors and employees are expected to fulfill all assignments without the assistance of their peers. As a result, they will not seek the assistance of their peers even when it is most appropriate to do so, or jeopardizes productivity and effectiveness.

Promoting a unified command is facilitated by clear missions within a limited time-frame where the challenges as well as the rewards are potentially significant. These conditions are often explicit in a military mission, a special law enforcement assignment, or a highly visible organizational project. Organizations need to create challenging conditions in order for employees to rise to the occasion, and to develop the right environment and the proper sense of purpose.

4. Unified Effort and Culture

A unified effort and culture results when all managers and employees are wholly engaged in the accomplishment of tasks needed to fulfill commonly shared organizational goals. As such, it necessitates a common understanding and respect for the mutual worth of all. It involves a commonly acquired set of knowledge, beliefs, and behaviors by managers and employees that is expressed in their sense of teamwork and views of fairness.

To build a unified effort and culture, managers must have the discretion within structured limits to reward and discipline employees swiftly and to correct problems without delay or fear of prejudicial recourse (such as invalid suits against managers). When there is a unified effort and culture in a successful organization, there is a genuine relationship of mutual respect between managers and employees. Employees feel confident and trust to freely give managers feedback on how they feel about their work, the balance of work among staff, the fairness of management, and about the responsiveness of management. Employees frequently bring ideas forward to management's attention on how to improve the organization. They want to take the extra effort to share their ideas to make a difference because they are proud to be a part of the organization.

A unified effort and culture means that employees can be stopped at any time and asked questions about the organization, its direction, goals, progress, or its management and employees, and the response would be open, accurate, positive and sincere. In addition, each employee tends not only to know the goals of the organization, but how their contribution fits into its success.

The characteristics of employees is that they: align their personal goals with those of the organization to the extent that they feel pride in and hope to share in its success; are more self-motivated for the good of the organization and each other; ask management for additional work when idle, suggesting work that they could do, or seek to help those that need help the most; and have interpersonal relationships that are friendly, positive, and work-oriented.

Where there is a unified effort and culture, team building comes naturally. Discussions of complaints by employees about other employees or managers are rare. Employees mostly talk about their work, the progress they are making, and are asking one another if they have any helpful ideas on how they can do things better. Personal experiences outside the job bring people together but personal problems are generally not discussed. When personal problems emerge however, the person in need finds real listening, caring, and helping. Informally formed groups of employees do not function as exclusive cliques, and are generally helpful not harmful for the organization.

Where there is unified effort and culture, employees understand, agree to, and follow policies and procedures willingly complying with high standards of performance and conduct. Employees feel energized by their work, and management-employee and employee-employee problems are almost non-existent. Employees feel their talents are being used appropriately and feel their work is very fulfilling. They sense that work has been distributed fairly and people are treated in an even-handed manner regarding rewards and punishments.

5. *Minimal Organizational Structure*

Structure is an arrangement of employees in a definite pattern to maximize results such as client service or product development. Structure in a successful organization relies on a minimal chain of command and span of control; a product or service workflow that occurs in the most fluid fashion with minimal disruption; with vertical and horizontal communication handled efficiently, where confusion and communication is minimized. When problems develop, the matter is quickly identified, understood and corrected; new management and audit review structures are not created to prevent problems that can be easily corrected.

A minimal structure is designed to fulfill organizational goals and facilitate optimal workflow and service delivery. Such designs properly align like-functions and minimize the span of control and chain of command needed for effective operations. While bulging organizational structures serve to isolate senior managers from employees, operations, and functional needs of the organization, effective minimal management structures can be designed only if top managers are willing to make necessary changes based on objective review. That is, structures should not be populated or formed from the self serving desires of popular managers; the vendettas of vindictive managers designed to isolate and destroy another competing manager; nor simply to allow a certain manager to acquire more status, power, or financial gain due to their association with the top executive.

A minimum structure does not have separated staffs or special assistants outside the chain of command that compete with managers over the power to influence, the power to provide information, and the power of position and authority. These staff and assistants are necessary only when the bureaucracy has grown too big to control, or in other words, is out of control. A minimal structure does not promote covert activities such as staff pulling rank on their immediate supervisor to complain to higher authorities in an effort of self-promotion.

In a minimal structure, all managers and employees know their responsibilities and are empowered to accomplish them, and are not afraid of being held accountable. It allows managers to appreciate the meaningfulness of their role within the organization, and enables them to feel a sense of accomplishment in the work they perform. A minimal structure helps employees feel they are truly part of a team ("one for all and all for one"). They are inclined to work hard, help one another when needed, show concern and emotional support when appropriate, and respond with spirited energy to achieve team goals. In such a structure, employees are kept well-informed and feel that they know what is going on within the organization, including how their performance level is being viewed and received by management and its external customers. Finally, a minimal structure facilitates the proper reward of managers and employees based upon merit, as effort is easily recognized and rightfully attributed.

6. *Simplified Workflow Process*

Workflow process is the way the primary product of the organization gets developed or services accomplished. Whether it is a production process or one involving service delivery, workflow in a successful organization is as simplified as possible but not simpler than needed. That is, there must always be sufficient quality and safety checks; a unit manager must not streamline to the detriment of the employees or company as a whole.

An effective workflow process keeps all managers and employees working in the most efficient manner to complete the product or service, with an open mind and focus on how to optimize value-added processing and service. That is, every effort is made to eliminate duplication of effort or unnecessary workflow processing, and how to add, subtract or modify steps that will greatly enhance the cost-effectiveness of product or service. An effective workflow process is organized in such a way to make optimal use of employees' skills and abilities, empowering them to make immediate decisions to improve efficiency, minimize unnecessary delays and disruptions, and toward transforming feedback from exceptional cases or failures into improvements to the work process.

7. *Built-in Accountability*

Accountability gives helpful feedback to managers and employees on the types of performance that both need for success and enable each to evaluate their own performance against measures of success within the organization. It is the ability to track and monitor manager and employee actions as they pertain to levels of organizational output or outcome; and provides the justification of one's existence within the organization. Accountability improves attitude, performance, conduct and overall value of the employee to the organizational mission and goals.

Accountability is not personnel evaluations that seek to

find deficiencies and weaknesses; rather it is the assessment of performance to help improve effectiveness. All-around accountability is the ability to measure and report multiple levels of feedback efficiently for the good of the organization. Managers and employees evaluate their own and each others' performance as it relates to the success of the organization. This leads to greater clarification of what is expected and how their combined work activities contribute toward meeting organizational goals, performance standards and higher management objectives. Accountability leads to continuous improvement in work processes, management performance, and employee/management relations.

8. *Technical Proficiency*

Technical proficiency is the ability of the organization to get highly technical work done efficiently. It means employees and managers have access to the most advanced equipment to facilitate a cost/beneficial operational process. It entails recruiting, retaining, and continuously providing employee access to the technical knowledge, training, and equipment to perform their duties at the optimally feasible operational level of performance.

The proper technical development level for an organization is based on a comparison of workload and process demands as weighed against costs and benefit/profit potential of the equipment. When the cost of technology outweighs its usefulness and effectiveness, an organization is not proficient simply by having the sophisticated equipment. An organization cannot acquire or maintain a position of leadership among competitors based on faulty investment assumptions. At the same time, an organization is not technically proficient if there is a failure to invest resources necessary to stay competitive in a business or service whose processes present a compelling argument for increased technical proficiency.

As an example, an organization is technically proficient if it makes wise and cost-effective decisions regarding the purchase of automated information hardware and software. It is not technically proficient when it utilizes antiquated database applications that are difficult to modify and maintain; if software development and maintenance is excessively costly; automated information equipment is unable to handle basic operational needs; and when employees are incapable of utilizing the automated systems for information, report generation, and decision making.

9. *Quality Input and Output*

Quality input and output are the incoming and outgoing materials, products or services that must consistently meet demands, needs and expectations. Quality inputs and outputs in a successful organization meet the highest standards of effective (non-defective), efficient, timely, and cost-effective materials, products and services.

Quality is achieved when managers and employees have high morale and satisfaction from their work, and look for ways to improve inputs and outputs continuously beyond acceptable standards, through direct and frequent communication with suppliers and customers.

Supplier and customer feedback from those who produce and use the products and services provided are vital. Just as an information technology staff should be accountable to internal users, a successful organization depends on receiving honest feedback from customers or service recipients and responding appropriately to it. When suppliers and customers are satisfied with the products, services, and relations, they show their appreciation by identifying, supporting, and voluntarily providing their input and feedback to improve the organization and offer referrals to expand the customer base or client service.

10. Effective Communication

Communication is essential toward keeping the organization informed, maintaining high employee morale, meeting supplier and customer/client demands, and ultimately in improving cost-effectiveness and productivity. Through advancements in Internet and Intranet communications, organizations can easily increase employee awareness and satisfaction and keep customers and clients informed, involved, and satisfied about organizational performance. Even with a minimal management structure, organization improvement can be stifled if employees are not allowed to provide their input on matters of importance or if they are not kept informed on management plans, decisions, and activities.

Minimum standards must be set up for communication within and between organizations to facilitate continuous input, feedback, and on-going improvement. Effective communication includes devising rules for communication to meet goals, to effectively use e-mail and the Internet, to conduct structured meetings through conference calls, and provide performance updates. Structured rules for communication minimizes waste of time as employees are consistently kept informed enabling them to focus on the day-to-day objectives for enhanced productivity.

Ten Organizational Priorities (TOP) Model Theory

The TOP Model Theory developed here is that:

- All complex organizations share a common rank order of priorities and without an understanding and commitment to the principles that are associated with this ranking, organizational and program cost-effectiveness will decline.

- The most important priority is to have quality top and senior management in order for complex organizations to succeed.

- All priorities of the TOP model are

interdependent and change that is most effective flows from the top down and back (1 to 10, and 10 to 1).

- Change in one area will affect change in the subsequent immediate areas down the rank order in a chain reaction.

- Management and organizational success depends on constantly striving to improve cost-effectiveness.

Each priority area has the strongest interdependence with its nearest priority areas. The area immediately preceding and subsequent to any single priority area being changed, will affect and be effected by it the targeted area for change. Organizational improvement begins with quality leadership and flows naturally from there through the accomplishment of all organizational priorities. That is, a dedicated leader can set into motion improvements that proceed throughout the organization (TOP model steps 1 to 10) like a domino effect as long as their vision is clear and effort persistent. Leadership brings unified purpose and planning which leads to (and is supported by) a unified command. The unified command promotes a unified effort and a healthy organizational culture (and is supported by) an effective structure. The structure that is minimal in nature provides for a simplified workflow process (and is supported by) organizational accountability concerning employee performance. The emphasis on improved accountability leads to the enhancement of technical and automated areas that support operation, administration, and management. The technical proficiency enables quality output in terms of cost-effective products, service, and performance. Quality output leads to and is sustained by customer satisfaction and feedback, which provides input for decisions by the organizational leadership.

The implications of the TOP theory are:

a) *Top executives, senior managers, and organizational consultants can use the TOP Model to better understand the "overall" organizational condition; can assess what areas need to be improved; and how to best make changes based on an awareness of these priorities and interdependencies.*

b) *Critical to organizational success is the understanding that improvement in any one area almost always depends on the improvement of the immediately preceding priority, considered a foundation priority, to support the progress proposed in the targeted priority. That is, when targeting one area there must be ample consideration given to the preceding and subsequent priority areas, as influencing and impacted forces, respectively. If not taken into account, any action taken in a targeted area may be misguided or backfire, with the improvement having difficulty taking hold or sustaining itself, or may fail due to the negative effects generated by or from the preceding and subsequent areas.*

c) *In order for organizations to be the best they can be, there is a need to continuously strive to improve cost-effectiveness. This is done through on-going assessment and improvements based on the TOP Model. Change actions should be initiated in any priority area where it can be demonstrated or observed that there are significant differences between the way things ought to be (based on criteria taken from the TOP model, from industry benchmarks, or from common sense) as compared to the way things currently exist.*

The Primacy of Priority Ranking and Relationships

The TOP model theory explains that organizational improvement progresses most naturally from step 1 to10 like a domino effect. The importance of the priority ranking and the strength of immediate relationships before and after each priority area is critical. This is perhaps better understood by taking it step by step:

Strong quality leadership affects everything in the organization but most importantly, produces unified purpose and planning and as supported by a unified command. The unified command promotes a unified effort and a healthy organizational culture and is supported by a structure that is not cumbersome. An efficient minimal structure provides for a simplified workflow process and is supported by organizational accountability and improved employee performance. The emphasis on improved accountability leads to and is supported by enhanced technical proficiency for the improvement of operations, administration, and management. Technical proficiency demands quality input and enables quality output which leads to customer satisfaction and feedback. This is supported by effective communication regarding products, service, and performance which leads to the strengthening of leadership and quality decision making, which closes the "negative feedback" loop of the TOP model.

Top and senior managers and high level consultants should take note that any improvements attempting to be made in one area without consideration for the relationship of the preceding step or also on its impact on the subsequent step is shortsighted. For example, making changes to the structure and workflow process will not be effective if there is inadequate personnel accountability and technical proficiency. The first step of the model (leadership) may be the most important for getting change moving, but it is not sufficient toward the making of an optimally successful organization. Also, a leader may be popular or held in high regard by their supporters, but they are not strong or effective until they assess organizational weaknesses across the TOP areas, and on a continual basis administer the proper improvements in all priority areas.

The change agent must remember that an organization cannot fully advance itself within any step without considering the interdependency and improvement needed within surrounding steps. It is difficult to take any step forward without realizing some improvements are probably needed to the previous priority area within the organization. Before fully implementing improvements within any priority, then one must at least look backward and forward along the TOP continuum and be prepared to offer recommendations toward each in order to build a foundation for viability within the targeted priority area.

Executives, managers, employees, and change agents can use the TOP model to assess the distance from "what is" to "what should be." Knowing what "should be" (i.e., the TOP model, benchmarks, standards, goals, common sense, etc.) is essential toward moving the organization to achieve system goals. Organizations that understand and use the TOP model will mature quickly into a successful open systems organization and be much more aligned with the ideals described in the TOP model than an organization that does not and typically remains operating like a closed system.

The TOP model can also be used to alert executives, managers and employees of the natural progression of change within any targeted priority area and properly orchestrate multiple layers of change at once based on the understanding of interrelated areas. The TOP model can be used to isolate areas for organization-wide improvement or be used by Unit Managers to conduct their own assessments and process reengineering and implement fundamental unit improvements. The natural aim in the TOP Model's application is to gradually improve the organization's or unit's cost-effectiveness.

If an external change agent is utilized, one might best begin the evaluative effort with understanding the organization's history and its existing state. The present state can be realized by diagramming and documenting the workflow process in detail as part of a study team consisting of people who work within the areas under study. This serves the advantage of helping to understand the workflow while gaining insights from those who can share their perceptions on what works well and where things can be improved. The use of change agents may not be the fastest way to make improvements but may be the best way managers can get honest feedback and it is why the approach is so frequently used by new top managers unfamiliar with the organization, its managers and employees.

Chapter 2

Cost Effectiveness: Making an IMPACT

The primary purpose of managers should be to continuously improve production and program operations. To do this, managers need to enhance operational effectiveness and efficiency, increase timeliness, and most importantly, improve cost effectiveness. In the private sector, due to the profit motive, businesses are naturally inclined to continuously attempt to improve cost-effectiveness. In the public sector, however, there are underlying forces such as the drive for organizational perpetuity, manager and employee self survival, and manager empire building that work against efforts to improve cost-effectiveness.

Certain types of managers in government resist any and all objective evaluation and accountability, and actually personally prosper in their careers despite contributing to its waste, mismanagement, and frivolous spending. Moreover, the problem in the Federal government is that the each general government reform mandate has not only failed to create improvements, but has actually increased the very problems it was intended to resolve. While such reforms may be initiated with good intention, the outcome of implementation has made government less effective, more expensive, and less controllable. Layers upon layers of reform initiatives have become part of the vast government bureaucracy without any accountability as to what was intended to be accomplished.

The IMPACT Model

In the TOP Model described in Chapter One, the second most important organizational priority identified is that of having a "uniform purpose and plan." This priority is addressed in some detail in this chapter by what is described here as the "IMPACT Model." The IMPACT Model stands for the *integrated management* (IM) of efforts to "*plan, assess, correct, and track*" (PACT) programs and work processes. This "pact" also represents the agreement that is made between managers and employees, to commit as partners to excellence in performance and integrity.

All organizations are challenged by both internal limitations and constraints and external demands that affect the ability to implement an effective PACT. The goal is to find the best solution to overcome these challenges. The IMPACT Model provides ideas for working within the existing organizational situation to make organizations more cost-effective in spite of current organizational deficiencies and challenges, inappropriate organizational structures, lack of high quality manager leadership, competing manager personalities, poor communication, and insufficient management guidance. In other words, IMPACT will make an impact in any organization that gives it a chance to be implemented.

Every employee, theoretically speaking, from the top manager to the lowest entry level employee wants to contribute to the good of the organization. The *integrated management* process identifies a series of strategies and tactics that when applied in earnest will not only make a real difference in overcoming problems, but will help the organization continuously improve cost effectiveness.

In a typical governmental organization there may be many pieces of a structure in place that emulate a type of IMPACT Model. Some of the parts are mandated by the Department, OMB and Congress, the overseeing authorities of the organization. Other parts are developed within and by the organization to fill in the remaining gaps of the structure needed to be effective or to make practical sense of the duplicative and overlapping mandates by the higher government authorities. A full picture of what might exist today is presented below but at the end of the chapter, a critique of the Federal government's efforts is noted, with the hope that a simple expression of the IMPACT Model is all that is truly needed.

The **"planning"** segment can consist of:

- Strategic Plan and a list of the Top Executive's Priorities;

- Strategic Advancement Forum (SAF) involving the top manager and senior managers to implement and track implementation of plans and initiatives;

- Resource Management Steering Committee to translate plans into resource allocations;

- Unit Performance Plans (UPP) for each unit manager;

- Internal Controls Corrective Action Plans for each program manager; and

- Documentation of program and business processes, in narrative and flow chart format, and major data indicators on plans, internal controls objectives, and standards.

The **"assessing"** segment involves:

- Program Risk Assessments and Evaluations and Unit Manager Self-Assessments;

- Inspections/Audit Staff reviews; and

- Independent testing by outside financial audits or by outside governmental units.

The **"correcting"** segment includes:

- Implementing the Strategic Plan;

- Implementing the Top Executive's List of Top Priorities;

- Implementing A-123 Internal Controls Corrective Action Plans;

- Implementing Program Managers' and Field Unit Managers' Performance Plans;

- Documenting all managers' corrective actions taken as needed; and

- Documenting the results achieved by consultant support services.

The **"tracking"** segment can consist of:

- Program performance reports (annual, quarterly, monthly/biweekly, and ad hoc daily reports);

- Program and Field Unit Managers' Performance Updates (via Web pages);

- Quarterly Status Reports (QSRs) for top managers and Cabinet oversight executives;

- Human Resource status updates; and

- Internal controls and audit corrective action plan updates.

The **IMPACT** effort is working as it should only if the

answers to the following questions are in the affirmative:

- Is each part of the PACT functioning effectively at all management levels?

- Is there some overarching authority (such as the Management and Planning Staff described in Chapter 8) to ensure a coordinated system of implementing PACT over the long run?

- Are plans, assessments, corrections, and tracking done consistently well and on time?

- Is system feedback on the health of the process given considerable attention and interest by top management?

- Is work evenly distributed, such that resource decisions affecting the positions, FTE, and budgets of Headquarters and field units based on objective performance data?

- Are work requirements for all positions clearly defined with performance criteria, standards of performance, and the path to advancement identified?

- Are annual statements of performance produced that demonstrate program cost avoidances, savings, efficiencies, and effectiveness?

- Does the performance data and organizational climate survey indicate that actions taken are resolving issues and problems?

The IMPACT Model Theory

The IMPACT theory for complex organizations is that:

- **It takes an "integrated management" (IM) effort, where all managers and employees are earnestly engaged in the common purpose, to develop and implement a strategic plan effectively.**

- **The IM effort not only brings managers and employees into a *pact* with each other, but brings the elements of "planning, assessing, correcting and tracking" (PACT) into a cohesive living enterprise throughout the organization. In order for "planning" to succeed, there must be an "assessing" of problems in performance, and "correcting" is facilitated by careful "tracking" of the implementation of plans. The plans become alive as results from the implementation bring about new plans and assessments. When the integrated management of planning, assessing, correcting, and tracking (IMPACT) is successful, it becomes the driving force in continuous organizational improvement, leading to better decision making, as well as cost avoidances, cost savings, and the ultimate**

goal of on-going improvements in cost-effectiveness.

The implications of the IMPACT theory are:

a) *Most strategic plans fail in development, and an even larger percentage of plans that become operational, fail in implementation. There are many issues in the development of Plans and in its implementation that need to be considered if it is to succeed. A strong IMPACT structure can provide an organization with an effective planning and implementation process.*

b) *The "integrated management" process involves the effort to ensure that planning, assessing, correcting, and tracking is working effectively and is fully integrated within the management decision making processes of the organization. Even when the elements of PACT are implemented, however, it may not operate effectively if program or field unit managers are allowed to ignore their responsibilities toward integrated management because they are "too busy" or view the effort as an "extra bureaucratic burden." Only when everyone is engaged, from the top executive to the least ranked of employees, does this pact between management and employees result in continuous organizational improvements in cost effectiveness.*

Implementing IMPACT

Planning

Planning is the setting down of purpose so that maximum available organizational energy and actions press forward toward that common end. Plans can be stated in quantitative or qualitative terms and delineated into goals, objectives, and strategies resembling long term, intermediate, and short range time periods, respectively. Plans can be put into immediate action items based on existing resource levels. The inherent beauty of plans is that it helps to best organize energy and actions so that savings and cost avoidances can be realized and become organizational assets instead of losses. At that point, these gains can be reinvested, used as profits or dividends, or returned to the customer (lower prices/unit) or taxpayer.

Plans considered as "strategic" are often those that are long range in outlook. The primary use of organizational strategic plans is to consolidate management thinking on goals into one document. This helps provide a picture as to where the organization is heading, and enables all levels of managers and employees to understand where the organization is going, and what needs to be accomplished in each mission area. The effect of a strategic plan is to reduce confusion, needless debate and discussion, and instead focus manager and employee attention on devising ways to more efficiently and effectively accomplish the objectives and strategies cited. A good strategic plan turns dysfunctional energy into a constructive force by unlocking resistance and refocusing organizational spirit toward a common direction that unifies organizational purpose, command, and effort.

Strategic Planning Considerations: A good strategic plan will energize program managers in the implementation of tactical plans and action plans to meet strategic goals. It can also help to instill a healthy element of competition among program managers that adds synergy to the implementation process.

Strategic Plans are likely to succeed if they are well received by managers and employees at all levels of the organization; supported as the official blueprint or road map for the organization's future; and appear to be instrumental in inspiring a positive response by all to move full steam ahead with its implementation. This occurs when we strive:

- To request input from all managers and employees, and this call for ideas must come directly from the top manager in the organization.

- To allow the flow of input to be received directly into a central database to be viewed only by the top manager, or as delegated in strict confidence to a support staff (e.g., the Management and Planning Staff). That is, the input must be received without potential intimidation and constraints felt by the normal chain-of-command. The input may or may not be anonymous but all employees must feel they are able to freely participate without repercussion.

- To ensure that the format for submitting ideas should reflect the structure and appearance of the eventual plan. For example, if the Plan will include goals, objectives, and strategies, then the sample input format for idea submission should include the same in order to foster full development of an idea by those providing the input and thus minimize misinterpretation by reviewers. This will enable good concrete ideas to be submitted and remain in its original state, with little revision. A solid raw idea or one submitted with great care can be the best form of input, and often should be adopted, not diluted through rewording into a consensus opinion. The process of transforming input received into the output of a final product will be minimized if instructions are clear and there is hope that good ideas will remain unchanged.

- To automate the reception of the entire feedback process provides better insight on the source and reason behind the idea, as well as its application. That is input analysis that generates a count of how many employees supported a particular idea, from what organizational units, and from what mission areas can be helpful in determining its benefit for inclusion into the final plan.

Planning must be infrequent and not difficult in order to avoid fatigue among the managers as well as employees. The process of transforming input into a useful product is a tricky business. Many like to discuss their ideas but avoid the writing process. Thus, there are common obstacles to overcome in the process developing a plan. For example, in addition to feedback from all employees directly, it is imperative to involve program and field unit managers for input, and to encourage them to solicit input from their own employees as well (even though employees are able to submit input directly via a central data base to the top manager or support team).

Each program and field unit manager can be asked to provide their vision for their own program or unit areas. In addition to considering the ideas, feedback and vision from within the organization, the plan must consider the external environment, including the context of the Department, OMB, Congress, and the Public. Thus, the plan will also need to accommodate clients or customers.

Strategic Plan Development: The actual development of the plan from this collection of input can be staffed as a group assignment to an existing "planning" staff, given to a special workgroup selected from individuals representing a wide range of mission oriented areas, or given to a single trusted individual with a sufficiently in-depth background of the entire organization.

The writer must have knowledge of the past and an awareness of what ideas have been tried previously, under what conditions, under which leaders, and within what structure. The writer must know something about the abilities of the current managers, the limitations of the budget, and the built-in constraints of the present organizational structure. Knowledge of the past and a keen awareness of the present is essential in developing plans that will realize their full potential in the future. Basically, a plan must read well, speak with a single voice, and inspire a positive response from all to get it done. For the most part, this is best accomplished by a single individual, if it is possible. To accomplish this, the individual must:

- review all the input from the unit managers, steering committee, program managers, and employees;

- conduct interviews with top management;

- analyze the ideas and consider their sources as well, understanding the vested interests and general negative characteristics of certain managers (some who will want to empire-build; others who will ignore difficult issues they are responsible for; and most who will resist all efforts to be accountable to performance measures such as cost-effectiveness);

- be able to balance the competing organizational missions knowing the relative importance of each mission without losing the support of any program manager;

- factor in budget needs and demands as well as reorganization proposals, and translate all ideas into terms short and long term strategies that will improve the health and cost-effectiveness of the organization;

- examine, interpret, weigh and prioritize objectives and strategies to ensure that their rank order and sequence is written in a presentation that makes the most logical sense; and

- prepare a high quality plan that is cohesive, comprehensive, and completed in the shortest time possible, because the pressure and anticipation will be great from the outset of the effort.

The plan's author should remain anonymous, be protected from pressures from others within the organization, and be able to turn over complete ownership of the product to the Organizational Head. This top manager then must take total ownership and responsibility for the Plan and provide executive leadership in selling and ensuring the implementation of the Plan.

Strategic Plan Context: A strategic plan is a reflection of the top executive's vision. However consideration must be given to a broader audience. In a private corporation, the Plan should include stakeholders and the Board of Governors and its Chairperson. In government, the Plan must satisfy and be approved by the leadership of the Department, OMB, and Congress. The Plan will be referred to in any number of policy, program and budget documents that will be sent to the Department,

OMB and Congress. For these reasons, a Strategic Plan needs to be written with the idea of being informative to a broad audience as well as specifically in compliance with the higher authorities.

One way to address the concerns of higher authorities is to dedicate a special section in the appendix entitled "Supporting the Goals of the Department, OMB, and Congress." This gives the organization a chance to spell out what it is doing to support the Department's Strategic Plan, the President's Management Agenda (PMA), OMB's Circular A-123 on Internal Controls, and Congress' Federal Managers' Financial Integrity Act (FMFIA) and the Government Performance and Results Act (GPRA). If no attempt is made to address these things, it only risks slowing down the review process or precluding the Plan from getting approved.

Also useful for inclusion as an appendix in the Plan is a description of the approach, underlying rationale and timeline for its development and implementation. As much effort that might go into a Plan, it is important to remember that it is only a starting point for making improvements at all levels of the organization. In its implementation, better means may be found to meet the objective than the specific ways stated in the Plan. In such instances, the choice should always be made to implement the better, more cost-effective strategies instead of the stated ones.

Often strategic plans are used merely as a way to support the budget formulation process. After a couple of years of their use, if no additional resources are provided based on the Plan, then it becomes obsolete. The best strategic plans, however, are designed primarily or even entirely for budget execution, with an emphasis on doing the most with the resources already provided. Managers and employees can easily submit ideas that would require additional resources to implement, but the ideas that are most valuable are those enabling an organization to do more with less. These ideas will create improvements and efficiencies that will avoid costs, produce savings, and enable improvements in the quality of service.

Strategic Plan Implementation: In presenting the Plan, efforts should be made for simultaneous distribution to all managers and employees, via mailed hardcopy or Intranet access, and include a personal message from the top executive that points to the management initiatives that need to take place immediately.

The impact of the Plan can be measured by pre/post performance and survey comparisons. A good Plan can also help change attitudes and organizational cultures, measured by an attitudinal survey such as the *OPM Federal Human Capital Survey,* which is issued every other year and for example, can indicate if there is a significant increase in overall satisfaction or an increase in confidence in leadership or in the communication of goals and priorities. Social Climate studies and other forms of internal surveys can provide the same type of feedback.

Successful implementation of the Plan often includes

the:
- Assignment of Duties to Managers, and to Special Implementation Committees;
- Director's List of Top Priorities;
- Unit Performance Plans (UPP) for each manager;
- Strategic Advancement Forums (SAF);
- Resource Management Steering Committee;
- Internal Controls Corrective Action Plans; and
- Process Documentation of changes to program and business processes in narrative and flow chart format, and identifying all changes in internal controls.

The *assignment of duties* is necessary to clarify roles and responsibilities. Also, it is important to make clear that there will be follow-up meetings to provide feedback on the status of implementation. Every objective of the Plan is assigned to a single manager, except where this is not possible, and then special committees are announced to address the remaining objectives or cross cutting issues.

In addition, the Director should describe some of the first actions that will be accomplished immediately upon the initial actions taken to implement the Plan, and then also provide a short list of the highest priorities to be accomplished within the present year. This list of actions and *Director's top priorities* achieves the purpose of reminding all managers and employees of the special need to adjust their own unit priorities according to top management's ranking of priorities.

The Government Performance Results Act (GPRA) calls for government agencies to develop a five year strategic plan and annual performance plans and reports. Organizations provide input and feedback to these agency plans, but may also choose to construct their own strategic plans and annual performance plans and reports. Input to develop these agency and organizational plans can effectively come from *unit performance plans (UPP)*. A UPP provides each manager with the opportunity to develop their own unit plan, in support of the organizational Plan and Departmental Plan. The development of the UPP keeps unit managers involved and responsible for implementing local strategies in support of the broader plans and accounting for progress made on performance.

The Unit Performance Plans can be developed using a text friendly database system, which allows input to and access from all Headquarters and unit managers in the field. These managers were previously asked to meet with their employees and develop goals, objectives, strategies and performance measures in support of the organizational Strategic Plan. Once constructed, they then might be asked to update the status of their own plans quarterly, and advance new plans and objectives as desired and existing ones are accomplished.

A *Strategic Advancement Forum (SAF)* is the meeting of senior managers and their support management team with the top managers of the organization. The objective is to review plans and implementation on a regular basis, focusing on money, people, and performance. SAFs are implemented as an effective way to monitor and support strategic plan implementation. These meetings are designed to hold senior managers more accountable for meeting their own performance goals and keeping unit performance plans in line with the Plan. The meetings enable senior managers, program managers, field managers, and committee chairs to discuss the strategies used to plan and implement objectives, overcome obstacles, and assess best operational and business practices. Peer pressure adds synergy to the meetings and boosts subsequent efforts to improve, as each manager is effectively being held accountable to top management as well as to their own peers, the other senior managers.

SAFs allow information to be discussed openly and objectivity where peer pressure and open accountability provide insight on who is doing their job effectively and who is not. The facts do not lie. Each manager is given a chance to describe their progress using quantitative and qualitative data to reflect their present implementation status, and how they plan to respond to immediate setbacks and future challenges ahead.

The ***Resource Management Steering Committee (RMSC)*** is a group that may or may not be needed depending upon the organizational structure and/or the degree of success attained by the SAF. The RMSC is composed of a few key budget oversight staff that are linked to budget decision makers within top management. This Committee ensures that the Strategic Plan and its implementation as well as the work of the

SAF are fully integrated into the budget decision making process. The RMSC focuses on providing feedback on actual spending against a current year spending plan (Budget Execution Plan). This Committee accounts for current year requests for funding and staff, and seeks to analyze the justification based on their own knowledge and research. For example, they may ask management and budget analysts (who oversee the program or budgets of requesting program managers) for an account of their independent recommendations, analysis, and justification. The Committee hears each request made by senior managers justifying program increases, and after an assessment, makes recommendations to the Director/DD on the request, factoring the needs of the entire organization, and the priorities set within the Strategic Plan and the Director's priorities.

This Committee also can support the SAF, tracking plans against implementation, providing the detailed reports on the impact and status of money, people, and performance. It adjusts budget execution plans against actions and budget formulation proposals accordingly. This Committee reviews the unit performance plan results of the senior managers and keeps top management informed in their preparation for the SAF on what the managers want to achieve, how they want to achieve it, and when it will be accomplished.

Internal controls are those mechanisms within an organization that safeguard against problems of fraud, waste, abuse, and mismanagement. Where there are vulnerabilities and weaknesses, new controls are designed to correct these situations, overcome problems, or strengthen the safeguard. In general, the cost of controls should not exceed the benefits derived from it. Where needed, Internal Controls *Corrective Action Plans (CAPs)* are developed to help focus and sustain the implementation process. The plan includes a status report and details the nature of the problem, the strategies and actions needed to overcome the problem, and the dates of projected and actual implementation.

The documentation of vital *program and business processes, in narrative and flow chart format*, provides an organizational baseline toward accounting for the impact of change. It is an essential the vehicle for measuring the impact of Strategic Plan improvement efforts. It is also the key for managing any planning and implementation change from an existing state to a future state, in an orderly fashion. Process documentation should include links to policy, procedures, and performance standards, and should identify all internal controls. As plans are implemented, the documentation is updated and records are maintained. The documentation serves as a reference for employees, a learning guide to new employees, and an assessment tool for auditors and management consultants.

Assessing

The assessment of performance, problems, and issues should be an on-going process in organizations and in a corresponding manner works hand-in-hand with the development of plans. Each year Federal government organizations for example, undergo a series of assessments to ensure that plans and missions are being accomplished and internal controls are being followed.

The organization has no control over reviews coming from outside the organization, but can assert some management of them by requiring all reviews to be coordinated centrally from a single point of contact. This reduces the duplication and unnecessary reviews, and facilitates the coordinated staff response to reviews.

The types of reviews conducted consist of three basic types: program reviews; financial audits; and information technology and computer security reviews.

- A "program review" assesses the status of program progress at meeting goals and objectives; whether the program is managed, structured, and organized effectively; and if policies, procedures, and standards are appropriate and being followed.

- A "financial audit" assesses whether financial management policy, procedures, and standards are maintaining internal controls to achieve the objectives of effective and efficient operations, reliable financial reporting, and compliance with applicable laws and regulations.

- An "information technology and computer security review" examines compliance with the *Federal Information Security Management Act of*

2002 (FISMA) and reports on the condition of information security controls regarding all general and specific applications.

The primary government oversight authorities for most government organizations include the organization's reporting agency or Department; OMB; and Congress.

***Department* reviews consist of:**

- **Management and program consultation reviews.** These reviews are usually conducted by a Departmental oversight staff (e.g., Management and Planning Staff, Evaluation Staff, or Program Review Staff), on the initiation of the Department Head, or on the request of OMB or Congress. The organization's management/planning staff can also initiate their own study efforts based on where the greatest need is perceived toward improving efficiency or effectiveness.

- **Financial operations compliance audit reviews.** These reviews are conducted by the Finance Staff with subject experts examining the financial records of organizational units and determining whether all information is in proper order and supports a smooth generation of financial statements and reports.

- **Information technology and computer security reviews.** These reviews are conducted by the Departmental Information Technology-related staffs via subject experts and outside consultants that examine the compliance of organization operations with hardware, software, communications, and security as measured against standards set up by Congress and its Government Accountability Organizations (GAO).

- **Independent financial audit reviews and program reviews by the Office of Inspector General (OIG).** These are two different types of reviews. The independent financial audit reviews are conducted by the OIG through a contract with an accounting firm, which examines the processing of all financial-related paperwork and automated transactions to determine if financial statements and reports are valid and reliable. Program Reviews, on the other hand, is an examination of program operations against goals and are conducted by independent management consultants or OIG program audit review staff.

- **Independent financial audit reviews by a central Departmental internal review and evaluation office.** These reviews consist of much the same as the OIG independent financial audits and the audits by Departmental Financial Staff, but are specifically designed to fulfill Departmental compliance to internal controls. These reviews are the result of agencies being responsible for overseeing Department-wide implementation of OMB's A-123 on Internal

Controls, including Appendix A, and Section 2 and 4 of FMFIA.

OMB's **management review consists of:**

- **Reviews with the Performance Accounting and Results Tool (PART).** The OMB budget examiners use a 25 point survey called the PART to evaluate overall organizational performance, including purpose, planning, program management, and program results. The examiner uses the answers to self-reported surveys from program managers and the documentation they attach as evidence to support their answers, to generate a score and evaluative opinion on the program. Each program is scored on these four review areas and overall, then OMB recommendations on improvement are issued, and following this, organizational corrective actions are reported through budget submissions.

Congressional **review consists of:**

- **Reviews by the Government Accountability Office (GAO).** The GAO conducts program reviews of organizations based on questions generated by members of the Senate and House of Representatives. The reviews cover the full range of possible study approaches as might a Departmental program review.

In addition to reviews by the Department, OMB, and

Congress, organizations conduct their own internal reviews. These consist of annual self-assessments by Headquarters' and district office management, and the periodic objective reviews by the organization's compliance review or internal audit unit. These

Organizational reviews consist of:

- **Headquarters Self Assessments**. An annual Risk Assessment Survey is administered as a self assessment instrument designed to review program management and internal control conditions within a broad program area. It includes, for example, questions on policy and written procedures, goals and accomplishments, internal control safeguards, checks and balances, automated program reporting on operational data, personnel resources, program administration, external program impact and interaction across organizations, recent evaluations or audits, or recent instances of errors or irregularities, effectiveness of existing controls and overall risk assessment.

- **Field Unit Self-Assessment**. A Field Unit Self-Assessment is conducted in each district covering all areas of management, operational, and administrative activity. It includes, for example, financial management, procurement, contract utilization, human resources, time and attendance, accountable property, motor vehicles, other equipment accountability, training, information technology (IT), IT security, and personnel security.

- **Audit Reviews**. The internal audit staff (often called the Office of Compliance Review) conducts periodic reviews of all district offices (about every four years). The review covers all areas of responsibility, including management and general office administration, operations and specific administrative compliance to policy and procedures, and the adherence to performance standards. These reviews are intended to provide a full picture of the operational condition of the district, both for the record, and so that corrective actions can be taken where needed.

Correcting

Correcting is a wide range of actions that ensure missions are accomplished, plans realized, and organizational purpose fulfilled. It means righting the wrongs and errors of past and meeting internal control objectives by taking necessary corrective actions. Correcting also means continually working to improve efficiency and cost-effectiveness of operations. Signs of correcting include:

- Planned program improvements being implemented;
- Performance data showing enhanced productivity, efficiency, and cost-effectiveness;
- Corrective action plans meeting targets on time;

- Ad hoc program corrections being initiated as needed, rather than delayed or avoided altogether;
- Coordination being initiated between and among organizational managers without prodding by top managers;
- Managers proudly displaying weekly and monthly accomplishments on the organizational website;
- Noted satisfaction of client, customer, and/or service delivery recipient; and
- When needed, readiness to contract for special support to assist in areas of organizational weakness.

Planning and assessing are intended to promote an inspired and organized process of organizational mission accomplishment. All the planning and assessing is meaningless until correcting takes place. That is, sometimes planning and assessing get in the way of correcting, if "paralysis by analysis" takes hold and issues that need to be fixed go unresolved, as options are endlessly considered, and future direction of the organization is left being uncertain, precarious, or stagnant. Correcting involves deciding what action to take and then acting to implement.

The fulfillment of organizational mission is also steered off track if planning and assessing is not done at all, or if done, is not used in the decision making process. Planning and assessing phases are done to support organization correction, and this is accomplished only when these prior phases are meaningful, clear and inspiring. Plans and assessments that include input from managers and employees tend to be followed more closely and implemented more vigorously than those that do not. The correcting process, then, is dependent upon planning and assessing being well done, as the better these are done the higher the probability for successful mission accomplishment.

Organizational Controls: Organizational controls are also needed for the correcting process to succeed. The *Revised Circular A-123, Management's Responsibility for Internal Control,* implemented in FY 2006, and derived from the *Federal Managers' Financial Integrity Act of 1982 (FMFIA)*2 defines responsibilities for internal control, strengthens the requirements for conducting control over financial reporting, and encourages internal control assessments to be integrated with other related management and program review activities.3 It emphasizes that "management is responsible for establishing and maintaining internal controls to achieve the objectives of effective and efficient operations, reliable financial reporting, and compliance with applicable laws and regulations."4

OMB's A-123 Circular requires Federal managers to "take systematic and proactive measures to:

---

2 Federal Managers' Financial Integrity Act of 1982; 31 U.S.C. § 3512.
3 Memorandum to the Chief Financial Officers, Chief Operation Officers, Chief Information Officers, and Program Managers, Subject: Revisions to OMB Circular A-123, Management's Responsibility for Internal Control, December 21, 2004.
4 Ibid.

- Develop and implement appropriate, cost effective internal control for results-oriented management;
- Assess the adequacy of internal control in Federal programs and operations;
- Separately assess and document internal control over financial reporting consistent with the process defined in Appendix A;
- Identify needed improvements;
- Take corresponding corrective action; and
- Report annually on internal control through management assurance statements."5

Additionally, *FMFIA, Section 2 and 4*, requires organization heads to review their own organization and "assure" the agency head that internal controls over program and financial activities are being properly maintained. *A-123 Appendix A, Internal Control over Financial Reporting*, also requires the organizational head to "sub-certify" that adequate controls are in place for accurate financial reporting. A consolidated agency report is then produced, entitled the *Performance and Accountability Report (PAR)*, whereby the Departmental Head provides the President and Office of Management and Budget (OMB) a summary of the overall status of agency operations and controls.

The problem with the A-123 and FMFIA is that there are no instructions, nor standard methodology, that describes what is required to ensure compliance with its objectives, or what is needed in order for component

---

5 Ibid.

heads to assure the objectives have been reached. For that reason, three primary criteria are developed here for rating whether the Organizational Head can assure and certify that the organization meets the internal control objectives: This strategy also incorporates a myriad of other overlapping Congressional initiatives and OMB mandates, all attempting general government reforms, to produce the most efficient and cost-effective organizations.

First: It must be demonstrated that top management places improving program performance and developing strong internal controls as a high priority;

Second: It must be demonstrated that a program like an "integrated management, planning, assessing, correcting, and tracking" (IMPACT) process is in active operation and is producing improvements in the primary core areas needed for any large organization to be cost-effective;

Third: It must be demonstrated that specific highlights from A-123 (and associated laws and regulations) have been implemented appropriately. This includes that:

- no material weaknesses have been identified internally by management or internal audits, nor significant problems identified by independent reviews by GAO, OIG, and Departmental oversight staffs (e.g., Finance, IT, etc.), that are without corrective plans in place for the correction of such problems;

- business processes and controls have been documented and tested;

- financial statements and related reports, as well as substantiating documents, are produced in a complete, accurate, and timely fashion;

- information technology systems and users operate effectively and securely, in compliance with overall FISMA/FISCAM objectives; and

- there are no significant lapses, with the exception of those caused by resource shortages, in implementing controls and corrective actions as needed in a timely fashion.

Therefore, for an organization to meet all three standards of performance, it must be demonstrated that top management places improved program performance and internal controls as a top priority; that there is a planning, assessing, correcting, and tracking process and it is operating effectively throughout the organization; and that no significant new problems were identified to date in the various assessments and management reviews conducted, and that problems previously identified have been corrected or are scheduled to be corrected. Additionally, the organization must meet the overall objectives for business processes and internal controls documentation, financial statements, FISMA/FISCAM, and timeliness of corrective actions.

Based upon this, the top executive of the organization is

able to provide reasonable assurance to the Department Head that the organization is in compliance with OMB Circulars A-123, *Management's Responsibility for Internal Control*, A-127, *Financial Management Systems*, as well as to the *FMFIA, Section 2 and 4*. The meeting of these standards also provides the justification for the top executive to certify to the Department Head on organization's compliance with *OMB Circular A-123, Appendix A, Internal Control over Financial Reporting*.

Tracking

Organizational tracking is the formal accounting for all significant aspects of the implementation of missions. Significant aspects include the monitoring of program performance, expenditures, implementation of initiatives as planned, and taking corrective actions as planned. Tracking involves the collection of data on all areas of correcting (noted above) and developing and presenting performance and management reports. There are many types of tracking reports, each serving a unique purpose. These reports may include:

- **Organizational Performance Reports**. Program performance data reports on the daily, weekly, quarterly, and annual performance on mission accomplishment and resource expenditure of the organization. It may also contain highlights of significant actions in summary narrative form.

- **Budget Reports.** Prepare budget requests and respond to budget request queries to the Department (April-July), OMB (August-January), and Congress (February-September, and beyond based on a Continuing Resolution). Quarterly Status Reports are also provided to the Department on the status of current year program performance and budget execution, and supplemental budget requests as prepared throughout the year based upon new demands placed on an organization as a result of Department, OMB, or Congressional initiatives.

- **Resource Allocation Reports.** Special reports identifying current vs. needed staffing and resource levels for Headquarter and district offices. These reports are generated following a data review of all district operational and administrative duties and the calculation of staffing need based upon standards of performance for all categories of work.

- **Decision Support Reports.** These reports provide a comprehensive status report on HQ program or district unit staffing and resources, workload and performance, time utilization by mission, status of accomplishments within unit plans, and environmental issues.

- **Unit Performance Plan Reports.** Quarterly updates of the implementation of program or unit initiatives proposed in the Unit Performance Plans.

- **Corrective Action Plan Reports.** Special reports on the accomplishment of corrective actions planned in response to specific concerns identified by internal, external, or self-reported audits.

- **Manager Webpage Reports**. Program performance and results placed on organizational website by program managers for all employees to view;

- **Employee Attitude Surveys.** Annual manager/employee surveys on organizational climate to assess the overall health and morale of the organization, as well as the communication and satisfaction experienced in offices.

- **Decision Follow-up Reports.** Periodic follow-up reports providing a status update on the implementation of decisions or requests made in major meetings by top management, such as during a Strategic Advancement Forum, weekly senior staff meeting, or financial management committee meeting.

Each type of report has a different purpose and a different audience. Together these reports provide a comprehensive picture for top and senior managers, as well as program and unit managers, to manage the organization effectively. The bottom line of all reports should point to cost effectiveness, or how much core missions are getting done and at what cost. Getting to this in a consistent way, capturing all costs for a service, and tracking it over time reveals the true success of the organization and its management and management processes.

Integrated Management efforts, by its very nature, enable many of these reports to be drawn electronically from basic data sources and compiled from a single database that tracks management information (often called a "decision support" database). Data from each program or district database feed the decision support system directly, so information is current and able to be displayed in graphs, charts and any number of report arrays. The integrated management effort facilitates the generation and use of reports and makes the decision making process more rational and based on real time information.

Tracking is critical to correcting, and is vital input for planning and assessing. Tracking contributes to motivating managers and employees to achieve success in organizations. The private sector has proven this to be the case over and over again. Federal Express, for example, has made this point clear within its delivery service showing how its ability to track delivery has transformed the company and now virtually assures timely arrival of its shipments. Tracking performance then is also important toward ensuring continuous improvement.

Tracking is also important for human relations. For example, tracking survey results on employee perception can help management understand and respond to employee morale issues, management and employee relations matters, and can help ensure there is congruity with management on organizational goals, policy, and performance. A social climate survey can detect problems between managers and employees and prevent dysfunctional outcomes by helping senior managers know what actions need to be taken. For example, an manager with an arrogant attitude, or one who discriminates against those of another race, or has a heavy handed authoritarian management style, may never have a chance to be a successful manager unless they change their ways.

Implementing IMPACT in the Federal Government

The *integrated management of planning, assessing, correcting and tracking* organizational effort requires that all activities described above are centrally coordinated and managers and employees are kept informed and involved. This takes considerable coordination of action and the full support of the top executive and to succeed it must make perfect sense to all participants, and have pay off in real results toward improved cost effectiveness, with innovation and risk taking incorporated into the mix.

For IMPACT to have the greatest effect, Federal organizations need independence from duplicative

Federal program requirements. For example, in the area of program review, more coordination is needed between Departmental, OMB, and Congressional sources to see what each other has already done to minimize any duplication of effort, particularly in the review of internal controls and the financial operations. Some would say the required financial statements themselves add little value to pre-existing OMB financial reporting requirements because the Federal government is simply not at all like the private sector. There is a need for financial audits but these audits can be accomplished within the organization for a very limited cost. Presently, the effort applied to get a "clean" opinion from the OIG and their independent outside financial auditors is extremely excessive, with no cost seemingly being too much to spend if it will orchestrate a favorable result.

Because of the emphasis on and need to obtain a clean audit, so not to be embarrassed, Departments have been led to create their own special review staffs to supplement those specialized staffs within the OIG. Staffs have also been created within Departmental Finance and IT staffs. Thus, four new staffs are sometimes created within an agency just to generate financial statements and reports that few if any program managers ever see or use. Additionally, each bureau, division, and office within Departments also construct staffs within their Finance and IT areas and sometimes their management and planning areas, to respond to the demands for financial statements and related audits. Each of these staffs may also contract for outside consultant support in relation to these efforts to assist with audit preparation, liaison support, and corrective action implementation.

All these costs of staff and outside help have been invisible to Congress and seem immune from review and accountability. Yet to date, after a decade or more since implementation, there have been few if any tangible benefits gained by the creation of these financial statements and independent financial audits. Moreover, and aside from the tremendous added cost, these efforts have often been counterproductive as the statements tend to obscure the tracking of program costs by organizational missions, disabling the view of cost-effectiveness.

Also, in the area of program review, the efforts by GAO and the OIG are too ill-defined, costly, untimely, and unhelpful. In most instances, their general approach is to highlight the highly unrepresentative perspective of a few people they have interviewed, or present highly generalized yet insignificant data as if it is mainstream thought or is of significant meaning, when it is not. Typically, these groups recommend improvements that are already underway, and present them as if they were the first to think of them. The problem is the supervisors reviewing the reports in the GAO or OIG do not have the background, experience or education to judge the organization's perspective on certain issues, nor the facts to judge the study approach, analysis, and conclusions. They cannot adequately assess the quality of the study but need to make conclusions and recommendations.

Also and in similar fashion, the OMB performance and budget reviews, as well as the PART review, lack depth and are weak, unsubstantial, and subjective. Generally, OMB examiners lack the background and experience to judge the programs they oversee for program and budget purposes.

Instead of all the meaningless oversight, government organizations should have a small program review staff that conduct useful research and review, and provide objective reports to outside examiners including the Department, OMB, and Congress. The studies would be streamlined, timely, and improve the chance for cost-effective improvements, savings, and cost avoidances. The current financial audit and financial statements and program reviews or program performance reviews, as directed by OMB and Congress would no longer be necessary. The cost savings would be significant, as would the increased program cost-effectiveness.

Chapter 3

Process Review: Establishing Continuous Improvement

By way of introduction to the subject of process review, Hammer and Champy[6] sum up some of the not so pleasant characteristics of many American corporations that they studied in the following words:

"Inflexibility, unresponsiveness, the absence of customer focus, an obsession with activity rather than result, bureaucratic paralysis, lack of innovation, high overhead--these are the legacies of one hundred years of American industrial leadership.....and,

If costs were high, they could be passed on to customers. If customers were dissatisfied, they had nowhere else to turn. If new products were slow in coming, customers could wait."[7]

The authors coin the term "process reengineering" (PR) as one approach to address these problems, and define this as the:

---

[6] M. Hammer and J. Champy. *Reengineering the Corporation.* New York: HarperBusiness, 1993.

[7] Ibid, p. 30.

"Fundamental rethinking and radical redesign of business processes to achieve dramatic improvements in critical, contemporary measures of performance, such as cost, quality, service, and speed"8....and adds that

"Reengineering rejects the assumptions inherent in Adam Smith's industrial paradigm--the divisions of labor, economies of scale, hierarchical control."9

In essence, process reengineering focuses on workflow processes and favors alternative work structures.

The TOP model favors minimizing organizational structure (priority 5) and simplifying workflow processes (priority 6). These priorities within the TOP model frequently serve as the central jump off point for organizational improvement efforts. They are centrally located like a fulcrum within the TOP model, and according to TOP theory, work in either area would naturally affect other interrelated nearby priorities of the organization. In particular, changes in the workflow process often require prior changes in the organizational structure as organizational structure affects workflow, and moreover, the most productive efforts to improve organizations starts at the beginning and the end of the TOP model, not the middle. The reason is that without the right leadership and communication, efforts at process review and process reengineering will not be properly implemented and will be doomed to fail.

---

8 Ibid, p. 46
9 Ibid, p. 49.

Conducting Process Reengineering

The assessment of need for organizational improvement is facilitated using the TOP model to compare current conditions and performance against an ideal state. The "what is" of the present is compared against the "what should be" as indicated by the TOP model. In conducting process review and reengineering, the following ten points should be considered, each reflecting or complementing some aspect of the TOP model:

1. Begin with the study of basic organizational purpose

Each priority within the model can be examined as applied to the target organization to see how each is working to support the organization's basic purpose, desired outcomes, and efficiency in meeting customer/client needs. The objective of executives should be to make their organizations be the best they can be, increasingly more cost-effective, while operating with utmost integrity and the highest ethical standards.

2. Seek to create the most cost-effective organization possible

Often the most difficult part of moving forward is the lack of imagination and the difficulty of seeing beyond the "Dilbert-type" work environment that often prevails in complex organizations. Employees and managers alike strive to free themselves from the senseless parts of organization activity, but somehow become enslaved to meaningless processes and confined within organizational structures that support inefficiency. The inability to see beyond the present reality makes fundamental change difficult. One often unwisely assumes managers will always be in certain positions, that processes only work the way they are presently, and that the division of labor and management configuration can only be as they are.

The more an organization compares itself against the ten organizational priorities, the clearer the vision of an improved future is realized, and the greater the potential of the organization to move toward fundamental improvement. Managers need to do more than just do things right, they need to do the right things. Using the TOP model can help get any organization moving in the right direction, the single most important direction, toward improving cost-effectiveness. Knowing something about what organizational components should look like using the TOP model is the start of progress needed to recreate how processes should be.

3. Consider how the relationship of organizational priorities affects the mix

To optimize organizational success, managers and consultants must pay attention to the strong interrelations within the TOP model. Success on one priority is not sufficient to ensure success on the next priority. Relationships between priorities are so strong that the success of any single goal is dependent upon the success of the step preceding the priority, and necessarily impacts the succeeding priority. In making organizational improvements, then, synergy will occur in a most noticeable fashion when two or three contingent priority areas are targeted for improvement at the same time.

4. Carefully develop teams and select team leaders

The success of process reengineering often depends on the generation of new team leaders within new flatter organization structures. The new team leaders respond with the energy and interest needed to boost the organizational productivity and forge new and improved relations with employees or clients, improving satisfaction and morale of both.

The success of teams, however, is often dependent on a common understanding of purpose, how they are developed and used (what authority they are given), and the special problems encountered and able to be overcome (how they work together to overcome obstacles). The application of teams can be very meaningful and beneficial but if not implemented effectively can revert to nothing more than reducing the size of work groups assigned to given tasks and result in lower productivity and morale.

Whether a work group is called a team, division, branch, section, or group, it is the size, function, and work process that makes the difference. When purpose is clear and the mode of performance is standardized, such as in an industrial factory, a manager can effectively manage hundreds of employees at a time. When clarity of purpose is ever changing as is the type of performance needed to meet rapidly changing objectives, then a manager may only be able to manage a dozen people effectively. This is the situation with the growing majority of occupations and services today.

In "service" jobs, a manager can achieve great things from a group or team of no more than twelve people. Give the same manager twice as many staff and the entire dynamics change. Now the manager or team leader must have two supervisors and as much as the manager tries to stay in touch with each person on the staff, they lose that direct relationship with employees. By selecting the proper group size for the nature and volume of work, staffs properly lead, can accomplish more in unique and creative ways and make greater contributions than staffs many times the size.

With each doubling of the size in the number of employees managed, i.e., 12, 25, 50, 100, 200, the manager becomes one full layer removed from the employee. This means that a manager with 12 employees has direct supervision, with 25 employees, has a layer of supervisors, with 50 employees has two layers of supervisors, etc. It is not so much the math but the concept that is important. The greater the distance of the top manager from the front line of workers, the more important is the need for extra modes of communication. Ultimately, the more employees feel appreciated by the top manager, the more inspired will be their work, and more attached and strong sense of belonging they feel to the unit/organization. This can be greatly aided through electronic mail that enables managers to stay in touch with all their employees without much extra effort than it may take to verbalize to a single employee.

The growing movement of work groups organized as teams is a function of the growing number of work activities that are service oriented in nature and in computerization of the workplace enabling fluid communications. More work can get done by a smaller number of people than ever before. Less time needs to be spent in meetings to stay informed because important information can be relayed easily through e-mail. The reference to "teams" is an important new name for work groups not only because it stresses the value of teamwork but because it emphasizes the new way work structure can be configured and functions performed. Computers enable people to work together well without working side-by-side and without physically meeting to resolve issues and set forth plans. This saves time and increases productivity.

The purpose in developing teams is to raise quality, productivity, and employee morale by reducing the vertical layers in the chain of command, not only raising the voice of potential leaders from the production area, but empowering all employees. The focus on teams increases accountability and winnows out existing managers that could better serve the organization in another capacity, such as providing a specialized technical service, being involved with customer services, or assisting another manager with special studies.

When team leaders come from within the highly respected and skilled ranks of production level employees, the position of team leader is respected as talented individuals are recognized by their peers and other team leaders for their performance. These individuals often become the brightest and best prepared leaders and future executives. Additionally, teams often work well as self-directed work units, provided most members' skills are on an even par and all members of teams are rewarded as a team. Teams work even better when team leaders can choose to abnegate their position of power with ease, and resume a non-management function adding to productivity, without penalty.

5. Carefully match employee strengths to organizational purpose

The successful development of teams through the reorganization of existing employees depends upon a close review of employee and manager characteristics. Teams should be organized in such a manner to ensure the collective good, and management must seek to balance the qualities of employees needed to best achieve organizational purpose. The match of individual qualities to organizational goals consists of grouping individuals that collectively have the following characteristics:

- *Capability:* consisting of the raw ability based on intelligence, education, background and experience to ensure functions will succeed and the brightest employees are used to accomplish the most complex and important functions.

- *Motivation:* employee self-initiative (that which exists almost regardless of the situation) should be assessed and balanced among teams but consideration must be given to intervening variables that affect motivation, such as type of work and work situation, management style and authority, and management relations and recognition of employees.

- *Vision:* the ability to see the big picture and to possess the right instincts, knowledge, and judgment regarding the direction the organization and the team needs to go in the future to be successful. At least one person should have a highly sophisticated vision of the future direction, able to integrate historical knowledge with practical judgment to make the right decisions almost instinctively.

- *Effectiveness:* the demonstrated ability to produce quality products or provide services efficiently to meet environmental demands. At least one person on each team should have a proven track record for maintaining a high standard for quality performance that will set the standard for the team.

Given that employee motivation and capability is high, the dilemma of the team leader is often trying to mediate or balance the strong personalities. Most of this depends on having a general understanding of how their employees tend to think. One who thinks in the abstract, for example the big picture dreamer, often has a problem breaking the whole into parts, working on the parts, and accepting responsibility for them. On the opposite extreme, the detail person has a problem putting together the whole from the parts. Basically, the abstract thinker has a problem with deductive logic while the detail thinker has a problem with inductive logic. Most individuals lean only slightly one way or the other but not to the extreme.

The manager needs to assign people to teams based upon knowledge of these traits which are considered differences, not weaknesses. Proper placement allows employees to use their traits wisely and makes others appreciate each others' unique contribution to the success of any effort. Without an understanding of the benefits and use of such traits, the manager will spend much time unlocking horns of these two types of individuals or between two of the same types in the extreme.

Some of the other corresponding differences found between types of workers that fall along the abstract or concrete dimension with some employees favoring abstract broad policy analysis, with general future and long term impacts, is creative, theoretical and big picture oriented. Others will have a concrete focus, relying on facts and technical details, wanting to know the immediate effects on narrow goals and parameters, being task oriented and expedient.

These descriptive terms aligned as bipolar opposites identify some of the competing values and potential conflict between employees within any team. The team leader works with all to draw out the best combination for the most cost-effective outcome. Both the abstract and detail person will be motivated toward results and learn to compromise for pragmatic reasons to produce a successful work product.

The team leader creates the milieu for the abstract and detail oriented to accept some cognitive dissonance and focus on a quality end product. Reinforcing extremes as a problem only stigmatizes the employee and further entrenches them, keeping them stuck in a fixed position. Instead the leader wisely includes them in discussions and treats as they would the ideal employee. It is often conflict generated from employees with extreme differences of approach that get the organizational unit to move forward in the right direction. Also, working through difficult processes helps all team members feel an inspired sense of unified vision and commitment to quality production.

6. Organizations need to strive for, and be always open to, continuous improvement

Process reengineering should not be considered a one-time quest for improvement, a quick fix. Process reengineering in complex organizations should be considered an on-going process, involving not just the improvement of a single part or several parts, but the continuous attempt to improve all parts. In order for organizations to stay competitive and improve cost-effectiveness, it is essential for the survival of businesses and critical for government, to keep the focus on continuous improvement. Significant one-time progress within any priority is not sufficient; optimal performance depends on continuous improvement on all priorities. Success within the first four steps may be enough to support a successful project or short-term mission operation, but long-term organizational success depends upon all areas functioning well and remaining open for further improvement.

Organizational improvement is tricky business. Government reform is particularly challenging. Efforts of the past have consistently failed and past failures have made future success only more difficult as failed change efforts instill a general reluctance to attempt future change. Any change introduced by Congress or OMB, for example, is immediately perceived with caution by managers. Anyone in the organizational chain of command can block something from happening. It takes a chain of consensus for an idea to move forward and it will only move forward if the top executive gives the official and personal "go ahead."

The forces against improvement are often daunting. This is because government often operates without serious review or clear measures of outcomes, has few or no competitive pressures to perform cost-effectively, and has little management support for changing the status quo since one is not typically evaluated on how much improvement they have produced. Also, in government, incentives for fundamental change are almost non-existent, the political risks always present as leadership is often penalized for leading. In fact, being exceptionally good and successful as a manager or employee is often viewed as a threat to higher authorities, who tend to focus more on power and control rather than on performance. The need for the application of the TOP model to government has never been more urgent.

7. Review leadership commitment to improvement

In any large company or government bureaucracy, there may exist institutional barriers that promote its own self preservation causing it to be sluggish, bloated, and unresponsive. The application of the TOP model can improve organizations by breaking the inertia and producing fundamental reform. The activation of teams and the development of competent team leaders from within the organization are often the means to reform. The team leader with front line experience knows the team members' skills and abilities and how to pool resources to meet the highest demands. Team leaders want to keep staff informed and involved in exploring new areas to which to make a unique contribution and to help set priorities. The involvement of team members in the organizational processes helps them be committed toward attaining high performance results and share directly in the rewards of their efforts. The byproduct is mutual respect between leaders and employees, top management and middle managers, and produces high organizational morale.

When organized into teams, the team leader often must personally make up for any area of deficiency among the team members. This means they fill in the areas of capability, motivation, vision, and quality production or pools resources in such as way that frees another team member to help out where lacking. The team leader must not only be the reviewer of work but be a team member that works where most needed. The objective of the team is to always do their best work and as much as possible prepare "complete" finished products in all that they do. Above all, the team will respond according to how much the leader cares for them, not just how much the leader knows and how hard the leader works. Employees always judge the heart of their leader by how fairly they are treated, honestly they are considered, and genuinely they are respected.

8. Examine impact and progress of technological development

There have been enormous advancements in computer hardware, software, telecommunications, networking, and wireless communication. These advancements have had a most significant impact on the workplace, bringing about major changes in the nature of work processes and roles, promoting the need to reexamine how and why work is done the way it is, and determining whether a better way is possible. A common problem within organizations however is rushing to automate processes without doing any prior process reengineering. As a result, much time, energy, and money is wasted automating present processes that further institutionalize operations that are inflexible, inefficient, and uncreative.

Advanced technology must be examined wisely and incorporated into the organization smartly, looking for all opportunities to improve, not hamper performance. Hammer and Champy have described some of the ways technology have helped performance:

- Shared databases enable information to appear simultaneously in as many places as it is needed, rather than in only one place at a time.

- Expert systems enable a generalist to do the work of an expert.

- Telecommunications networks allow businesses to simultaneously reap the benefits of centralization and decentralization.

- Decision support tools such as database access and modeling software enable decision making to be a part of everyone's job rather than a manager making all the decisions.

- Wireless data communication and portable computers enable field personnel to send and receive information wherever they are, eliminating the need for offices to receive, store, retrieve, and transmit information.

- Interactive videodisk enables direct contact with customer and diminishes the need for personal contact and expensive travel.

- Automatic identification and tracking technology enables quick and ready access to inventory or supplies rather than trying to find out where things are.

- High performance computing enables plans to get revised instantaneously rather than plans getting revised periodically.[10]

Thus, change agents (inside or outside the organization) need to include in their process reviews whether each technology is being fully and effectively applied.

9. Use outside consultants and in-house staff wisely

In government, service delivery is often a coordinated effort involving one or more divisions and branches, as well as Headquarters, regional, and field offices. Problems in the process are sometimes difficult to correct by just looking within one area or one part of the process, or looking in one direction up or down the chain of command. The employee, supervisor, manager, and

---

[10]M. Hammer and J. Champy. *Reengineering the Corporation.* New York: HarperBusiness, 1993, p. 92-101.

senior executive are rarely able to pinpoint where system change should be applied. Problems with service delay, process fragmentation, inadequate automation, poor relations, etc., can cut across all sectors and demand reviews of purpose, outcome, and customer/client focus.

Consultants and organizational change agents can provide a critical role to managers and top management within the organization. Using the TOP model, the change agent can provide a simplified evaluation measure that assesses the organization's degree of openness regarding all ten priorities essential for success and generate an organization profile. This approach focuses top management on the need for a holistic look at the organization's health. Although such a study is preliminary, it can identify priority areas that are in greatest need for a more comprehensive review.

This broad preliminary process review can provide the top executive an effective gage on the organization and prevent problems of implementation within any one step being reviewed later in a more comprehensive manner. That is, once the bigger picture is illuminated, forces within the organization effected and threatened by proposed changes in any single priority area, will be less likely to become resistant and "submarine" these efforts, if they are aware that broader change is imminent. Without top executive involvement, however, threatened program managers can sabotage any improvement efforts within any priority area before it can be fully implemented and successes realized.

To be optimally effective, outside change agents must receive the support of the top executive from the outset. They must also organize a study team that includes employees within the organization, keeping these staff highly involved in all aspects of the review. The outside "change agents" should perform the role of "facilitator" and the individuals within the organization should provide leadership and staff necessary. The commitment of leadership and sense of ownership by managers and staff will facilitate acceptance of study results and implementation of study recommendations.

10. Use TOP model for planning and assessment

The TOP model provides the framework for top management, middle managers, and employees, as well as change agents, to diagnose organizational problems, determine which step or cluster of steps is in greatest need of improvement, and provide logical recommendations as to what order of need and emphasis would be best to address the problems. Interestingly, outside change agents are often called upon to document known problems as evidence of the need to take action against a manager or staff already targeted for replacement or reorganization.

The use of the TOP model helps to examine the broader picture, and can be used as a guide to know if there is a need for a new manager or if there is something else that needs to be done. Sometimes the manager is not as responsible for poor performance as are other factors. The TOP model may show how things could get worse with a new manager even one with an excellent track record, because the entire situation within which the manager must operate is untenable.

During any assessment process, the full perspective of the organization must be kept in mind however narrow the lens may be for the sake of the immediate analysis. Even though the change agent (manager, employee, or consultant) may be assigned a narrow task to accomplish (focus on improvement of a single organizational step in the TOP model) they must understand something of the dynamics of the entire organization to succeed. Change agents can begin their analysis and primary focus for change at any step, but their efforts will not be as effective until the preceding or succeeding organizational steps are open for review and improvement, because of the interrelationship of each priority.

Process review and reengineering will lead to many types of change in the workplace. As Hammer and Champy point out, these might include:

- combining several jobs into one, and changing simple tasks to multi-dimensional work;

- empowering workers in many ways including making decisions; freeing managers and supervisors to be leaders, coaches, and cheerleaders rather than controllers, scorekeepers, and bosses;

- performing process steps in a new and more natural order, and perhaps, with multiple versions for different needs;

- conducting work where, when, and how it makes the most sense;

- minimizing checks and controls, and reconciliation;
- changing work units from functional departments to process teams;

- changing the focus of performance measures and compensation from activity to results, and cultural values from protective to productive; and,

- reducing organizational structures from hierarchical to flat.[11]

Essentially, as a result of process reviews, and by proper planning and assessment efforts, any number and type of changes and continuous organizational improvement can be realized.

---

[11]Hammer, p. 51-64.

Chapter 4

Top Management: Making a Positive Difference

The TOP model places top priority on top management, so it is essential that new top or senior management be the right person for the job. The top manager in business or government controls significant power not just over the organization but in many ways over the lives of all their employees. This can be good or bad depending on how the privilege is handled. If the new executive thirsts for expanded powers without concern for the consequences, for example, they will most likely not be a "good" leader nor govern in a way that is cost-effective for the organization and healthy for its employees. While all new executives want to make a difference and have a legacy, there are ways to go about it and ways to avoid.

The following are ten things to consider toward enhancing one's chance for success and ten things to avoid. Paying attention to these will greatly aid the reign and remembrance of these managers.

Considerations for the New Top Manager to Enhance Success

1. Know what to do and how to do it

More than anyone, the top executive has many

opportunities both to enhance the effectiveness of organizational mission and the working conditions and morale of employees. The top executive has the greatest chance to help employees meet the challenges of the job and make a positive difference. The attributes that may have helped the newly designated top executive to acquire the position, however, may not be sufficient for continued success. Wealth, charisma, status, personality, and networking may have helped get one into a position but do not assure a leader's success. Getting a position may require good style and form but making something of it requires leadership, and the full understanding and actualization (i.e., the form and substance) of the position.

The probability of success for the new political leader of an organization is directly dependent upon two factors:

- prior knowledge and experience and recent exposure to the organization, its environment, and its managers, including understanding their background and capability; and,

- prior knowledge and experience with the managing of improvements in organizations.

If the new leader has both a background in the organization and experience in managing organizational improvements, they stand the best chance to succeed. If the individual has subject-specific experience but no experience in managing improvements, or if they have experience managing improvements but no background within the organization, they stand about a 50-50 chance of being successful.

A new leader who walks into an organization without the benefit of knowing the organization and what to expect nor any prior knowledge and experience on how to improve an organization, is going to have a difficult time making a positive impact. These managers need to go slow, learn fast, and rely on people with such expertise and not just a few, to develop the wealth of information needed to fully understand the situation. Decision making instituting fundamental change should not proceed until one believes they are well informed and broadly advised having talked to many people at every level of the organization.

2. Leave your baggage behind

To "leave your baggage behind" means that you come unencumbered and that you are your own man. A new top executive should not bring a host of companions along and they should not come looking for others to carry their heavy baggage. If one looks for someone to drive them everywhere, escort them to meetings, arrange every meeting and personal introduction, they will soon lose their sense of independence and objectivity. Try not to look for what the organization can do for you, such as every company perk, but strive to find ways you can help the organization.

It is not unusual that a political appointee or a newly hired executive to walk into a position with little knowledge about the job. In an effort to learn quickly, the natural tendency is to look for help from those that appear well informed, non-biased and objective. For every new executive there are always several people ready and willing to convince this new top manager that they are just the pundits he/she is looking for. The unskilled top executive quite naturally forms associations with these pundits but unfortunately, often absorbs their outlooks and biases. Even with the best of one's instincts and intellect, advice cannot easily be critically assessed or scrutinized. Such information does not substitute for prior knowledge and experience about the organization and its environment, nor about how to manage and improve an organization.

It is difficult to run an organization and stay neutral and unattached while trying to buy time to digest all the information and make necessary decisions responsively. The new executive must realistically assess one's chances for success and yet at the same time not be discouraged. Self-doubts can be overcome through careful insight and action. The typical political appointee in government, for example, comes to the organization without background in the organization, without knowledge of a historical perspective on the organization or its managers, and most likely without the certainty of a single noble and loyal friend. As such they need to be very careful who they choose to listen to.

If they are given any briefing at all, it comes from those in positions of higher authority (e.g., Departmental oversight) that have strongly vested interests. These advisers ("wanna-be top managers") from outside the organization, usually minimally employed themselves, will strive to win influence at this very vulnerable time. They may know little about what is really going on in the organization, but they know more than the new chief executive, and most assuredly are intent on conveying a perspective that only they, the self-proclaimed pundits, can help the new executive fulfill critical needs of the organization. They claim to be familiar with the operation of the Department which must approve all budget and policy actions. These "informed" senior Department-level executives usually have little management experience and responsibility, have little or no influence in the budget or policy areas, and are the first people to avoid. In general, it is not wise to trust in outsiders who purport to know more about the organization than managers within the organization. Their perspectives are formed from a responsibility-free perspective that is easily jaded.

The next most dangerous individuals of would-be advisers are former associates or friends of the new top executive in need of an important management job. Although the top executive may feel indebted to loyal outsiders, they will need to understand the price in hiring them. From the moment the outsiders come on-board, they will be viewed with hostility and the new executive's stature will be diminished, crippled by the impression that he or she cannot make it on their own, and that they need a friend or companion "hold their hand." There will be acquiescence but distrust for these individuals until the top executive leaves. This will be the cue for the non-merited hire to find another job as well.

These types of outsiders bring a real danger to the organization, as their role is typically to uncover the real problems of the organization and provide feedback to the top executive. Nothing could be more difficult to find under such circumstances. Real managers and employees will have no part of the new comer, as no one would be less trusted than such a person who has no background or experience, can easily cause errors, misinterpretations, and miscommunication on so many levels.

In addition to rather natural insecurity and sycophantic personality, other characteristics of the "friends of the top manager" are their general deficiency in leadership ability which begins with not having a true interest in the organization, its mission and people. The tendency for these individuals who are "given manager jobs" is to build-up staff size with "newly recruited" staff to assure their own security of position starting with their own new loyal subordinates. At the same time, their regular employees' productivity and morale decline abysmally. Work products are designed primarily to make the manager look good; the idea of displaying an employee's work or showcasing employee/team efforts is lost. Decisions are made on the basis of personal security, not for the organizational good.

A third most frequent mistake made is for the new top manager to befriend the common complainer, who is usually articulate and convincing yet otherwise slightly deranged. These types will generate a lot of confusion for the top manager and waste a lot of their energy. The common complainer has nothing to lose. The realization of truth becomes an ever evasive commodity the more time is devoted to listening to these types.

Another problematic influence is the individual, inside the organization, that has a personal agenda or vendetta against another employee, manager, or senior executive. Such an individual sees the new top executive as the perfect opportunity, and maybe their only hope, to find the means to upend their personal nemesis. These individuals will latch-on to those newcomers close to the new executive to provide inside information to the new executive. They will try to influence the change they desire to pay back someone for the wrong done them. In some cases, the cause is just and warranted however, and the new top manager then becomes obligated to correct the wrongs previously done.

A new top executive who responds quickly to any advice or information without first investigating further and allowing others to provide their side of the story, will have a hard time overcoming the damage done. The new executive and new hires will be marked with failure; will be considered as aliens who are uninformed and "totally without a clue"; and solid managers will turn away wanting to be isolated from "guilt by association" and will instead entrench themselves for the duration. The long term consequences, by the time the political executive leaves two to four years later, is that the individuals who were brought over and the ones from within, the complainers that were promoted into management positions, will either be relegated to the organization's "Lost and Found" category for other managers to make use of as high priced staff, or will be fighting to retain their positions at all costs with the new top executive.

In short, a new manager should try not to bring "their" people into the organization from the outside as new permanent staff. Instead, they should just work hard to identify issues using their own skills and intuition, perhaps, work from within the organization as much as possible and if needed, bring in new highly qualified talent on the basis of merit, and use the remaining steps outlined below as a personal blueprint for moving forward.

3. Undertake an objective review

The effort to promote organizational improvement often begins within the first three months of a new top executive being on the job (or the "first one hundred days"). If the new executive is unfamiliar with the organization and its management, they might wish to rely on a trusted outside consultant for the preparation of an objective review that is used to supplement one's own intuition. (This consultant would have no interest in permanent employment, would need to be skilled in advising top management and would need to have some prior experience revamping complex organizations.)

If much is needed in the way of improving the organization, the top manager should remain non-committal about the future to all existing managers. The study is announced with the purpose being to better prepare the organization for the future. Typically with complex organizations, the major need is to downsize the management structure, giving emphasis toward greater decentralization. Some of the objectives of this approach are to:

- delegate more responsibilities and staff downward to field unit managers to improve production;

- shift the focus of attention at Headquarters more toward providing services and meeting the needs of the operational field units and away from regulation and control;

- streamline business practices, reduce unnecessary management layers, and increase employee commitment by expanding their authorities;

- increase management accountability for resource expenditures and program performance; and

- improve the effectiveness of strategic planning, performance planning, measurement, and monitoring, including program evaluation and review.

The announcement of these objectives energizes the

organization toward the exploration of better ways to do things and be organized. Despite all the distraction, commotion and complaints, the existing work will get done, and often it gets done within the same time and with even more quality than previously. This is a time when folks will do their best not just because they sense they are being watched carefully, but they want to reflect pride in what they do for the entire group they represent.

4. Ensure that employees at all levels have sufficient opportunity to provide input.

Also, during this period of study, the new top executive should maintain an "open door" policy, giving employees from all levels access to top management and the consultant to discuss organizational problems and concerns. The top executive should invite all employees to provide their input on problems, issues, and ideas for organizational improvement via memo, e-mails, and through televised town hall meetings for all employees. This is different from the isolated initiatives taken by bold or brazen individuals. This is giving each individual the authority to speak on behalf of themselves, their unit, and their organization, for the good of each.

An Advisory Committee staffed with internal planners needs to be identified that can help the consultant review the concerns knowledgeably and objectively. Field managers can meet with the consultant and the Advisory Committee in day-long meetings and prepare reports on their ideas. These groups of front-line supervisors are often the most helpful format for providing useful suggestions on a wide range of problems and issues that confront the organization. They can also be helpful in providing useful ideas regarding the fundamental reshaping of workflow processes and organizational structure. The TOP model can be used to provide the full range of essential areas and the emphasis should be to address the causes of problems and issues, rather than the superficial symptoms. This is a monumental task but if done properly can generate great insight on the many types of changes that are needed to vastly increase cost-effectiveness.

5. Review organizational structure and function

At a minimum, the new Top Executive must do a comprehensive review of organizational structures and functions including an analysis of:

- Organizational charts, and statements of the mission, functions, and staff size of all organizational units;

- Position-by-position descriptions of employee duties, grade/salary, position descriptions, personnel classifications, and reporting relations of all employees by level;

- Past year performance plans for organizational units and overall organization against year-end results;

- Business process flow charts in all program areas; and,

- Issues and problems that need to be resolved and program improvements that could be realized that have been identified through prior audits, reviews and evaluations.

- Any proposed reorganizations that have taken place or have been proposed over the past ten years.

6. Conduct program manager performance, accountability, and planning reviews

Once the Top Executive has had sufficient time to understand and absorb the organizational feedback, and specific structure and function, and program problems and issues, there is the need to give the senior managers a chance to have their say. Each senior manager should participate in a minimum of two in-depth interviews with the Top Executive. Before these meetings, all program performance data under the responsibility of each senior manager should be reviewed by the top manager, as well as prior program and financial audit and evaluation reviews, and any third party suggestions for organizational improvement.

The senior manager describes past performance and current plans. The top manager can ask each senior manager to provide a summary self-assessment using the TOP 10 model, and propose any changes felt necessary in each area.

7. Decide on the nature of organizational configuration needed

After all input is organized and assimilated, the top executive decides the type and extent of change needed. If the nature of change is only minor revisions affecting only a few people, then change can be swiftly decided and implemented. If it is going to take more than a little bit of tinkering, then a more formal proposal and plan will be needed. The complexity of the plan should take into account all concerns and likely consequences.

If a major reorganization is needed, a design may require anything from the changing of a few boxes to a conceptual obliteration of the existing organizational configuration, including the vestiges attached. That is, sometimes there is the need for fundamental change that alters the people, personalities and business practices that have "always been" or has "always run" a certain way. It may also mean erasing the current and pre-set notions about the present. One of the best strategies in accomplishing this is to compose a small work team to develop the new organizational blueprint. The group begins by setting the rules for building the new organizational configuration based upon the purposes listed above (#3) and ends with the generation of several alternative configurations that attempt to depict the most cost-effective organization possible.

8. Construct the best organizational option

The organizational options are designed using the following developmental steps:

- review consolidated feedback from all sources and detailed summaries of the interviews with the program managers;

- analyze advantages and disadvantages of the various proposals and ideas presented;

- brainstorm within the study team to realign the organization according to similar functional areas;

- consolidate similar functional areas and redefine the distinct missions and objectives of the newly aligned activities;

- use work process reengineering techniques to develop new workflow structures that would optimally utilize staff and resources to accomplish missions;

- reassign existing workforce and management structures needed to support the new functional alignments;

- identify and separate the functions that would be performed by Headquarters and the field units and define the vertical and horizontal interaction and decision making power within the organization;

- describe the critical transitional elements of the reorganization (e.g., phases 1, 2, and 3), in order to show how the organization will need to move from the current state to its future state of existence;

- develop new and internally consistent administrative, business, and operational structures within each core area to include program oversight, management support, and general and specialized service delivery; and,

- develop detailed organizational charts to account for all positions needing to be incorporated into the new configuration.

9. Do not dodge the tough decisions

There will be tough decisions to make in the placement and selection of people to manage the new structure of the organization. These decisions are just as important as changing the structure. As mentioned earlier, strong leadership is the first and primary step toward organizational success; all other areas needing improvement depend upon the leadership.

The tough decisions regarding program and personnel are critical to make if real problems are to be corrected. It will be necessary to replace managers that have gained and maintained their positions by abuse of others; have mistreated, unduly favored, or ignored employees they are assigned to manage; have continuously erred in their duties and performance responsibilities, have overspent or misused funds, misspent and failed to properly supervise contracts, repeatedly failed to meet plans, have failed to set goals, have declining cost-effectiveness results, or been unresponsive or have insufficiently served clients or customers.

Replacing managers is only one part of the corrective action that may be needed. The top executive should attempt to fully understand the management abuses and injustices from the past that have been ignored or fostered by past mismanagement. This will have great significance not only to such individuals that have been offended but to the entire organization. If managers are not replaced and if victims are ignored, the new executive will be aligning himself/herself with the managers that have mismanaged in the past, and the perception of all future positive actions will be tainted and diminished. This sin of omission and of enabling, which is a common wrong, will mean that the new top executive will become equally culpable when future problems develop or other retaliation occurs.

Moreover, while the reorganization effort is underway, there will be decisions that need to be made about ordinary but difficult daily business. These decisions should not be dodged just because significant attention is being focused on the reorganization activities. Be sure to discern which decisions can be delayed and which ones need to be delegated to competent and trustworthy senior managers. Do not task a manager that should be replaced for wrongful behavior with new responsibilities, as if successful performance will provide redemption for past wrongs.

10. Develop rules for an orderly transition

A transition plan needs to be constructed before the release of any comprehensive reorganization package. As part of this plan, there should be a structure designed to keep the organization informed on the transition process through the lengthy and full implementation of the reorganization.

Negative Effects of Excessive Central Control

Try to remember as top manager, there is a great need to practice humility. It is very easy to act like a "ruler" rather a servant. Many new top managers fail when they think they need to assert their power to prove their superior position. It is easy for the new top executive filled with a sense of power derived from their position to seek ways to demonstrate their vast influence and control. To cement their authority, they often decide to develop new policies and assign new regulatory powers to their own internal investigator staff which will report directly to them, the new top manager. They may start off by establishing a new policy that requires "all complaints and allegations" be reported to the inspector's office, committing to investigate each reported allegation, and encouraging reporting.

While this may sound like a fair and noble idea, one that could only be interpreted as worthy in the eyes of all employees, the reality produces grave unintended consequences. The problem is the new policy to centralize all complaint review undermines the power of middle-managers who can address and resolve problems quickly, and indirectly effects productivity in numerous unanticipated ways. Moreover, the lack of definition as to what constitutes a legitimate complaint means it can be broadly or narrowly interpreted based on subjective review and a judgment of "misconduct" can be arbitrarily applied to anyone accused, the target of the complaint, rather than isolated and determined on the basis of the facts of the case.

The centralization of power through internal investigations is the most common mistake of new inexperienced and particularly insecure managers and as such deserves examination. While such policy may be rationalized as an effort to right all wrongs, it almost always is revealed later to have been devised with devious intentions and in a thirst for greater control. The effect of such policy impacts the entire organization, not just those who are targets of investigations. The more serious negative effects on the organization caused by this excessive desire to control will be shown by the following effects on management, employees, inspectors, and the organization.

Management Effects

The way an organization dares to discipline itself has

significant impact on the human relations and performance of the organization. Policy centralization, where only a few people control disciplinary decision-making, does not enable discipline for misdeeds to be administered in a fair and equitable manner. The top manager can with little consideration for alternative solutions remove managers or individuals in critical positions "for cause" other than performance (i.e., unstated minor misconduct), as a way of trying to further enhance their own power. Those on the lowest levels of the organization are often held to the highest standard, given less flexible resolution options (if given any options), and receive the most serious discipline.

Employees and some managers (especially those targeted by the top executive) are "dragged through the ringer" to prove false complaints that may have been offered anonymously and motivated out of envy and selfishness. As a result, managers become too scared to correct staff conduct and performance problems because they are afraid they will be filed against, particularly when it involves a minority or female employee. Instead of counseling and correcting the individual, the issue is referred to Inspections. Instead of the matter being resolved by issuing immediate, fair, and effective discipline, providing re-training if necessary, and letting the employee get on with their job, the matter takes many months to investigate and resolve, causing additional costs or workload backlogs.

Without disciplinary authority, managers are without power, and this creates an atmosphere where there will be more misconduct and more allegations made. Employees know when managers have real power and control and they act according, with respect and obedience as appropriate, and they immediately know when the opposite is true. When all complaints are reported to Inspections, managers are not involved in some of the most fundamental decisions affecting their employees and lose the opportunity to correct staff behavior through a balanced measure of control and compassion; and the entire organizational unit loses a chance to learn and grow together for the better. Managers who lose such oversight responsibilities, act less responsibly, and do not risk getting involved to resolve related issues in support of employee justice, integrity, and service, as apathy takes hold.

Employee Effects

When given power, direction, and protection of top management, inspectors are likely to lose perspective of reality, "attacking" each complaint or allegation as if a serious problem, blowing them out of proportion to their actual significance. Employees being investigated respond to this inflated seriousness as threatening and naturally become defensive. In their fear and anxiety, they challenge the system by lying about their offense or falsely claiming sexual or racial harassment, as a justifiable defense, sometimes beating the system, but more often becoming victims of the process. Essentially, inspectors scare offenders into believing their offense is more serious than it is, and instead of telling the truth and taking their punishment, employees decide to lie or cover-up. When caught, they receive harsher punishment, even removal or firing from the job not for the offense but for the lie.

In the case where the individual is fired, not only does the individual lose his or her job, but there is the obvious system loss of investment in the individual's prior recruitment, training and development. This amount can exceed $100,000 over the initial two years of employment. Rather than further investment in the individual, the pervading rationalization is that the system is "cutting its losses" before incurring greater losses in the future.

Another concern is that powerful inspectors taking an "equally" serious review of all complaints and allegations may overlook the worst offenders. For example, smooth talking employees can often evade the inspector's indictment, even when both the manager and employee know they are culpable. The inspector's investment in a lengthy and costly investigation is for naught, while the employee misses the opportunity to honestly confront and learn from mistakes made and the chance to change. As a result, an employee with a problem that could have been confronted and disciplined by the manager has an increased likelihood they will commit a more serious wrong in the future.

Inspector Effects

When the inspector decides to investigate all complaints and allegations as equal in significance, it causes the caseload to increase beyond control, expands backlogs, lengthens time for completion of investigation, reduces inspector morale, and increases inspector burnout from work overload. Most importantly, it changes the inspector's approach toward one of being more aggressive during interviews in hopes to get quick admissions of guilt or denial. This approach increases the risk for lying, which is cause for dismissal, regardless of the seriousness of the charge. When inspectors cannot investigate every allegation, they must be able to distinguish the cases quickly where actions were premeditated and driven by motive, as opposed to those actions that were the result of impulse, poor judgment, or accidental in nature.

The number of quality cases by inspectors will decline when the emphasis of the inspector office is on productivity measured by how many cases completed. The greater the importance given to the quantity of cases, the less the importance is given to the quality, value, complexity, and true significance of cases. As a result, the perceived status of the inspector's office will decline with the rise of closures of significant numbers of minor cases that should have been handled quickly by managers.

The aggressive behavior from inspectors creates its own repercussions. They become labeled as "headhunters" and "junk yard dogs" that are more inclined to "go after" people in their investigating, and fail as "watchdogs" serving to protect the organization from serious intrusions. As much as some inspectors will be sensitive to this and try to avoid conducting themselves in any way that might reflect these images, they become inescapable victims when the system asks them to investigate allegations that are really too minor to warrant their efforts. As a result, they often become locked into their jobs and locked out of other jobs, stigmatized and distrusted by all. Managers hold animosity toward them and other employees believe these inspectors will never be able to be team players. If given a new position, former inspectors can expect that their job will be made unnecessarily difficult. Filling jobs of inspectors, in contrast, becomes difficult as well, due to the perceptions of this image and the intolerable job conditions.

Organizational Effects

An overly ambitious Inspections staff reporting to the Top Executive with every complaint and allegation has wide ramifications and pervasive negative impacts on other aspects of organizational behavior. Often, the result is that employees become pitted against inspectors, managers, and each other in a "win or lose all" contest, in which the organization never wins, and where self-protection and manipulation displace organizational achievement and effectiveness. The new top executive that uses Inspections to gain greater control produces an effect on the environment of unit management that can be characterized either as "separated-isolated," "terror-ridden," or "conflict-filled."

Separated-Isolated Environment:

The emphasis on total centralized control can cause an isolationist environment at the local unit level where employees come to work with the sole intention of getting through the day "with their noses clean." Here employees exhibit the very real concern that if they do anything wrong, however slight, they will be reported to the Inspectors office. This breeds isolationism, lack of teamwork, a "see no evil, hear no evil" mentality, where employees are content doing their minimal routine work, drawing a paycheck without any enthusiasm for their job.

In this environment, there is a disincentive on putting forth extra-effort or doing anything creative or generating new ideas for improvement. Individuals do not have to perform well, they just have to make sure they do not do something wrong. Mediocrity in performance becomes better for ones long term survival even if it is not good for ones' mental health. Close ties to people, or being energetic or innovative is dangerous, for it separates oneself from the norm and makes one a target for someone envious, who will work the system against them, i.e., find a reason to report them to Inspections.

In this type of environment, morale is poor and employees lack a sense of togetherness. The atmosphere is missing the humor, vigor, fun, and the greater sense of caring for one another. The organization suffers from an inability to grow, being productive is not a part of the culture, and team work, often the necessary ingredient for success, is lacking. Managers and employees do not want to get involved because they fear they might get hurt "by the system." Managers are scared to be managers and are not comfortable directing, correcting, and disciplining. They also do not want to invest themselves in caring and cheering on their employees. In short, they fear challenging or correcting employees because they do not have any power to discipline and are continuously vulnerable for a complaint or legal suit against them. Managers are not being asked to be responsible for the very things they are being paid to do, manage people.

Managers however can easily abuse Inspections as well to get rid of the employees they do not want to be supervising, a kind of "workforce cleansing." Managers generally will not confront "problem individuals" honestly and openly but instead will wait until they get entirely "out-of-line." Once they can solidly show evidence and fully document an infraction, they will "lower the boom and nail" the targeted employee. The manager's problem that should have been dealt with by the manager a long time ago then becomes the inspector's problem to deal with much more serious ramifications.

Terror-Ridden Environment:

In the terror-ridden environment, the office resembles that of a war zone, where the basic mode of operation is one of pervasive on-going suspicion. Here employees and managers "keep book" on everyone and can be used as bargaining chips to cover themselves against abuse in the future or can be used as a way of seeking revenge. Because inspectors investigate minor conduct violations, employees and managers protect themselves by taking notes on others' behavior as their protection against others threats. The employee that has something on everyone is the one most secure in this environment.

In this environment, allegations are often not reported to the inspector, but are used as personal bartering tokens. This is why some of the most serious violations can very easily fail to be seen by the inspector. The pervading mentality becomes "I won't report on you, if you don't report on me." The person who reports to the inspector is not just labeled a "tattler" and forgotten but is one who can expect to get "wiped out" by counter files by any number of others keeping book. Once the inspection is completed, the individual that squeals gets the worst assignments, is given poor performance ratings, is withheld promotions, and is the most obvious target for other reprisal. Neither managers nor other employees care to protect them as they violated the code of conduct for office survival in the terror-ridden environment.

Conflict-filled Environment:

In the conflict filled environment, there is a clear demarcation between managers and employees and each class is at war with the other. Rather than a spirit of cooperation, with everyone sharing the same values and mutual concern, the atmosphere is filled with negative relations. Organizational behavior is characterized as adversarial, the "us against them" mentality. In this environment, decisions are consistently made to benefit and secure greater control by management.

With serious management-employee relations problems, the inspector fuels the animosity. The investigation is often a misguided venture with the focus misdirected and intended to deflect attention from real areas of concern, the conflict between management and employees. After the investigation is completed, little change occurs if management is at fault and excessive discipline is administered if employees are found culpable. The inspector's investigation is inclined to favor management, since the operation style of Inspections and top management are compatible, that is, is authoritarian in nature. Thus, limited focus is applied to the real problem of manager-employee relations, and no justice can be expected from the conflict-filled environment.

Chapter 5

Managers: Bringing Out the Best

Whether in business or government, managers want to know how to become more cost-effective and how to get more satisfaction from their work and create the ideal work experience. Managers who are trying to do their best should always be concerned with how they can be better leaders, to which employees will respect and respond earnestly in their work efforts. Managers are interested in the achievement of organizational and personal goals, and this takes a vision and plan that will lead to fulfillment and the results desired. One must constantly work on becoming an effective manager and the results will be most evident in ones' ability to make significant contributions for the good of the organization and toward the development of employees.

Essentially, to become an outstanding manager one must develop a firm understanding of the:

- business of management;
- employee motivation to perform; and
- "character" needed by managers to be truly successful.

The Business of Management

The manager's success largely depends upon decisions

made regarding three primary activities: planning, organizing, and controlling,[12] and includes:

Planning:

    1) Mission
    2) Goals
    3) Objectives

Organizing:

    4) Job Descriptions
    5) Grouping of Jobs
    6) Group Sizing/Assigning of Employees
    7) Delegation of Authority

Controlling:

    8) Standards of Performance
    9) Information on Performance
    10) Corrective Actions of Performance

Planning defines the desired ends and means (in the ultimate, intermediate, and short-run) for the organization and its parts. Organizing consists of defining how to arrange employees and lower level managers to implement plans in the most efficient

---

[12] J. Gibson, J. Ivancevich, and J. Donnelly. *Organizations*. Dallas, Texas: Business Publications, 1976.

manner. This involves describing organizational activities needed to be performed; dividing, coordinating, and distributing the authority and activities by manager and employee; and determining the size of staff by activity area. Controlling includes the setting of performance standards, internal controls, establishing audit checks and data systems to properly monitor actual organizational results against plans, and to take corrective actions when necessary.

While planning and organizing deals with getting things right the first time, controlling is the management mechanism used to correct faulty planning and organizing activities. If the engineering is not meeting design specifications, either the organizing activity needs to be reconstructed or the plans need to be rethought and adjusted. Essentially, planning is concerned with doing the right things; organizing is concerned with doing things right; and controlling is concerned with ensuring the right things are done right.

The manager must use diagnostic, administrative, and technical skills to be effective. The diagnostic skill is used to assess organizational problems and issues and set forth plans. The administrative skill is used to organize the personnel, work processes, and other activities for work accomplishment. The technical skill is used to oversee the work process implementation and ensure quality control.

The goal of getting the job done the best way possible to meet organizational goals and individual needs presents an interesting cognitive and affective challenge. The cognitive challenge is to find formal and informal structures that work best for performance, considering the characteristics of the employees. The affective challenge is to perform work duties in a manner that promotes the feeling of warmth, friendship, trust, interest, respect, and rapport among employees and between the manager and employees. The effective manager promotes a feeling of mutual trust (the affective challenge) throughout the process of performing major activities (planning, organizing, and controlling), and uses special skills (diagnostic, administrative, and technical) to help produce the best outcome for the organization and employees.

In many large government organizations it is likely that significant problems exist not only in organizing but also in the functions of planning and controlling. Very few management reform initiatives by OMB and Congress, for example, have demonstrated the positive effect intended and very few outcomes are even measured. When reform is haphazard and fails, the morale of managers and employees is diminished. When organizations make significant changes in organizing but fail to measure the impact on cost-effectiveness, performance and the corresponding costs of implementing change, the organization is uncertain if the reengineered process was really worth the effort.

Government reform actions have rarely focused on restructuring and downsizing. One exception was the National Performance Review (NPR) which called for the downsizing of management by setting standards and increasing the minimum number of employees supervised, empowering employees by reducing the number of approval levels of authority, decentralizing decision making, and establishing smaller work teams. Minimizing the vertical chain of command improves communication, empowers employees and maximizes available resources for the support of production and service.

To meet the NPR objectives, radical restructuring of government was proposed. For example, typical large governmental organizations have a minimum of four hierarchal levels:

- Top Management;
- Middle Management;
- Supervisory Management; and,
- Production/Service.

One approach would be to integrate the Top, Middle, and Supervisory Management levels into two levels. Consider the likely outcome. Middle Management at Headquarters would be eliminated (e.g., from 25 managers to 0) and Supervisory Managers could be reduced in half (e.g., from 64 supervisors to 32). In its place, Top Management would need to grow (e.g., from 3 to 10 individuals) drawing from all displaced managers to select the strongest leaders for the unfilled top management positions. The remaining managers would be shifted to provide direct field services, becoming part of production or filling vacant field management positions where they can add value to the product/service provided.

Unfortunately, in general, very little progress was made to meet the objectives of the NPR initiatives due to problems of implementation. The implementation process for how to organize to meet the objectives was never defined and organizations were left to create their own method for attaining the reform goals. Even with top executive support, the accomplishment of NPR goals largely depended on Congressional support and subsequent Administrations following through on implementing the initiative and sustaining it.

The Government Performance and Results Act (of 1993) was implemented to address problems of planning and controlling. The Act calls for Strategic Plans, annual Performance Plans, and performance measurement. It is yet to be seen if this effort will lead to the development of performance standards, internal controls, and feedback systems that will enable continuous improvements of the organizing activities within the Government.

The implementation of government reform have focused on organizational activities needed to comply with Government mandates, but successful implementation may be dependent upon improving managers' diagnostic, administrative, and technical skills and training them to meet the corresponding cognitive and affective challenges.

Employee Motivation and Performance

According the Abraham H. Maslow,[13] needs are arranged in a hierarchy with the highest needs, those with the most motivational force, being the self-actualization needs. The needs are:

- Self-Actualization (the need to fulfill oneself by maximizing the use of abilities, skills, and potential);

- Esteem (the need for self-esteem, and esteem from others);

- Belonging, social ties, and love (the need for friendship, affiliation, interaction, and love);

- Safety and security (the need for freedom from threat, i.e., the security from threatening events and/or surroundings); and

- Physiological (the need for food, drink, shelter, and relief from pain).

Maslow believed that the basic needs (e.g., physiological) would be satisfied before higher level needs and that once a need was satisfied it lost its potential to motivate. Because most people readily

---

[13] A. Maslow. *Motivation and Personality*. New York: Harper, 1954.

satisfy their physiological, safety, and security needs, Maslow contended that it is the higher level needs that serve to motivate the most. It is toward these higher level needs that Maslow recommends that managers turn their attention. When they are ignored, employees become frustrated and the sense of conflict of unmet needs lead to dysfunctional behavior.

Needs compel employees to set and meet organizational and personal goals. In the process of pursuing the setting and meeting of goals, however, employees can experience stress, frustration, and conflict if the organizational climate blocks their development. The resolution of the conflict either leads to behavior that can be termed "situation appropriate" or inappropriate. Inappropriate behavior includes aggressive and diversionary types of behavior that is dysfunctional to both the employee and the organization.

Employees respond differently to stress on the job due to past personal experiences (behavioral conditioning), genetic composition, cultural/ racial constitution, intellectual ability, interpersonal skills, and prior work experiences. Dysfunctional reactions to stress include anything from the fear of losing one's job, to the ruthless struggle to gain organizational power. The dysfunctional behaviors are the result of higher level needs being blocked or suppressed.

For the sake of simplification, Maslow's hierarchy of needs can be reduced to three broad but closely corresponding need areas:

- self actualization,
- social approval/esteem, and
- survival and security.

These three categories may be referred to, respectively, as: "we want, we need, and we must have." Certainly we "want" to be the best we can be for what we are individually called to be; we "need" social approval and esteem; and we "must have" physiological and safety needs met. We want, we need, and we must have are employee demands that managers must understand. Their awareness of this increases their capability to be sensitive to others, and helps them better relate to the emotional, social-psychological, and economic aspects of motivation.

It is useful not only to collapse Maslow's needs into three broad categories but also to redefine the substance of each need according to what each means within the work context. The following descriptive model is developed to serve as a tool for managers and organizational analysis.

Self-Actualization Needs

Self-actualization in the workplace consists of employees' perception of the following factors:

Autonomy: opportunities to make independent decisions, set goals, and work without close supervision.

Personal Growth: opportunities to increase ones personal competency thereby enhancing ones market value. This may include a wide range of things such as receiving modern training and equipment, or improving ones technical proficiency, leadership skills, clarity and accuracy of oral or written communication, self-confidence, emotional and intellectual ability, alertness, originality, integrity, etc.

Promotion Potential: opportunities for career advancement within ones organization.

Achievement Potential: opportunities to gain responsibilities and make an impact of significance through ones accomplishments and contribution of effort. This involves, for example, the ability to recommend or implement major organizational or work process improvements.

Job Content: intrinsic interest in the nature of one's work.

Social Approval/Esteem Needs

Social Approval/Esteem needs are defined in the workplace according to employees' perceptions of the following factors:

Relations with Manager: the degree of concern that employees feel that managers have for their welfare.

Relations with Employees: the degree of

concern that employees feel that other employees have with each other.

Feedback: the quality of feedback on work received from the manager (including the technical competence and respectful manner with which it is conveyed).

Recognition: the quality of recognition received from the manager on work (including the manager's responsiveness to adequately reward the better and harder working employees, as well as the manner it is done.)

Esteem: the feeling of self worth and confidence based upon how the manager and other employees respect ones position and work.

Survival/Safety needs

Survival/Safety needs are defined in the workplace according to employees' perceptions of the following factors:

Salary and Benefits: the employees' satisfaction and perception of fairness on the amount of wages and benefits paid for work performed.

Job Security: the nature of assurance given to employees by the employer regarding their job security.

Working Conditions: the employees' perception

of the health and safety of the work place.

Ten Hypotheses Applying Maslow's Hierarchy

With Maslow's hierarchy adapted for the work setting, the following hypotheses can be developed that have implications for employee motivation and performance.

1. The amount of employee need fulfillment at each level of the Maslow need hierarchy determines their overall level of motivation, satisfaction, and performance. The more the manager increases the potential for higher level fulfillment for employees, the greater employee performance and satisfaction.

2. The greater the manager's competence, motivation, vision, and quality productivity, the greater will be the employee motivation, satisfaction, and performance.

3. Self-actualization is considered as things the employee wants; social approval/esteem is what they need; and survival/safety is what they must have. This translates into survival/safety being considered an employee right; social approval/esteem being considered a much needed benefit; and, self-actualization being a much desired privilege.

4. The successful manager strives to fulfill employee needs and their success and own need fulfillment depend upon it.

5. Self-actualization is the greatest motivator and is most

essential to achieving employee satisfaction and performance over the long run. The greater the employee perceives danger of not meeting lower level needs, however, the greater the motivation and effort put forth on the short run, but the greater the potential problems in the long run.

6. The sum of all needs fulfilled as perceived by employees will not only be a valid measure of motivational force of employees but will also be directly related to organizational performance as well.

7. Organizational strength is the combined measurement of organizational performance and employee satisfaction. Organizational strength diminishes or increases in tandem with motivational force and ones perception of the fulfillment of employee needs.

8. When employee needs are blocked, there will be an increase in dysfunctional behavior such as aggressive responses (power seeking, open hostility, and unresolved conflicts) as well as in diversionary responses (avoidance, passive aggressive, defensive, rationalized behavior). When the highest needs are blocked, motivational triggers can only be generated at the next level of need satisfaction. That is, if self actualization is blocked, the primary motivational force shifts to social approval/esteem; with much more time and effort needing to be expended in this area by manager and employee. Similarly, when this becomes blocked, the primary concern becomes maintenance of survival/safety. Long term performance deteriorates as

each higher set of needs goes unfulfilled.

9. The power of motivational force increases when blocks are removed. The blocks may be mental, social, situational, pertain to one's ability, or even imaginary. The manager helps employees stay engaged in the pursuit of the highest motivational objective by including the employee in determining what contributions are most needed by the organization and by the planning and control of work activities. The employee continues the pursuit of their greatest needs by becoming fully engaged and centered on the work process through self-discipline and focus, and getting necessary training and education to improve performance.

10. When managers ignore their role to make a significant contribution to the organization, they will remain unable to fulfill employees' needs, and others will attempt to meet these needs. For example, when managers do not address employees concerns regarding salary, job security, working conditions (survival/safety), unions will form to protect employees. When managers do not provide quality technical supervision and a climate for quality interpersonal relations (social approval/esteem), then outside consultants will be called upon. When employees do not receive channels for achievement, recognition, the increase of responsibility, or the possibility of growth and advancement (self-actualization), then there is an increase of employee dissension, absenteeism, and turnover.

The Character of Managers

A strong organization is one who has quality managers (and employees). The key to the long term health and strength of the organization relies on its managers to look after the health and welfare of their employees as well as that of the organization. There are three types of managers but only one is successful at protecting the needs of both employee and organization. The three types are the:

- *"power manager"* who seeks power for its own sake and becomes ineffective motivators of employees as power for its own sake corrupts;

- *"employees' manager"* who is a successful leader that unselfishly seeks organizational and employee fulfillment, not power; and

- *"marginal manager"* who has lost their desire or who runs away from their responsibility to manage and fails themselves and their staff.

The profile of the power manager, employees' manager, and the marginal manager are presented and compared against the role of meeting organizational goals and individual needs.

Power Manager

The power manager is one who pursues power for the

sake of control and the assurance of one's own position and continued influence. The control of decision making and protection of one's own position far outweighs concerns for what might be best for the organization and particularly for those managed. As a power manager, the primary concern is staying in the position of power and the fear of losing one's position is reflected in every personnel action and program decision.

The power-manager wants all employees to submit their wills and total energy to carrying out their instructions according to specifications. Employee thoughts and opinions are simply not asked for. Questions are raised only to clarify the manager's request. Objections are raised only if the manager is known to have not considered an important piece of information or has received erroneous information. As a result, employees become a part of either the "in" or the "out" group. There are the loyal patriots, numbering about 25% and there are the other 75% or second class citizens relegated to lower tasks or exiled to secluded out-of-sight duties. The latter group of employees are unfulfilled, frustrated, silenced, and have been asked to check their brains at the front door. They have little involvement with the Power Manager, but they have not "sold out" as loyalists and puppets; at least their pride and dignity is in tack.

These managers want to be viewed as all-benevolent and generously reward those most compliant to their requests. The Power Manager attempts to develop employees to their fullest potential only to the extent that it might help them fulfill their own dream of empire building and self perpetuation. Staff is considered both personnel and "personal" resources of the manager, to help fill ego and relationship deficiencies.

The Power Manager treats employees with favoritism, according to a perception of who can produce the most and be most beneficial to their own success. The primary concern of the power manager is having a loyal, hard working staff that helps the manager with their personal projection of "looking good" to their superiors. They approve only of employees who know their place and defer their opinions to the better judgment of the power manager. Employees are viewed as personal "chauffeurs," helping the manager get somewhere or as "toads or caddies," that can walk along or behind carrying the manager's heavy bags, keeping opinions to self unless specifically asked. "Yes sir" or "yes madam" are the words most spoken by these employees. The phrases most spoken to the manager are "that's a great idea," or "I was just thinking that myself."

The Power Manager most guardedly controls all channels of feedback to the top executive. This involves controlling all discussions that employees have with their superiors so as to avoid any negative feedback from below surfacing at a higher level. Lower level staff that have creative and independent ideas for organizational improvement are considered adversaries and threatening forces to the Power Manager. Such ideas must be controlled.

Even if the underling has ideas that are supported, they

are not welcomed until the Power Manager has had time to co-opt, rename, and absorb all the credit for the idea. Such innovative ideas will be advanced only after the Power Manager has had sufficient time to totally control all angles of the idea, particularly the presentation for approval by top management. This usually is only when the idea has laid dormant for a lengthy enough time that it can no longer be associated to its original source. The Power Manager finds an opportunity to use it to their advantage, as if it were an original idea of their own, and waits for the right moment that the top executive could use the idea to salvage a poor record of performance or resolve an imminent problem that could have long been avoided had the idea been presented earlier.

An underling that tries to pursue an idea without the Power Manager's approval is considered a renegade, a challenger to their position of power, and is either transferred into a position of no responsibility or is simply ignored. The issue is one of power and control, not of agreement or disagreement. As stated above, it does not matter how good the idea is for the organization, until the originator is displaced, replaced, or forgotten, the idea lies dormant. The Power Manager deals swiftly with individuals who break the chain-of-command, because they know full well the potential implication of an "end-around," since this is most likely how they succeeded in obtaining their own position. They most likely befriended the previous top manager and at the right moment convinced the top executive to initiate actions to find a "better, more useful role" for the good of both the manager and the organization. Once the boss is removed, this individual is "asked" to assume the position in an "acting" capacity as an extra duty, to which after a few months of "stellar" performance, is given the position officially.

The Power Manager is one who seeks to control power sources among peers and subordinates including areas such as decision making, influence, information, and money. They exercise tight reign over the spending of current year money, by setting low thresholds for review and approval of spending. This way they can exercise complete control over daily decision making, appearing as an everyday Santa Claus by being the only one that can spend money and give out the "goodies." They also attempt to hold tight control over planning and information. This way, they can hold on to the important vantage point for being all-knowing and God-like. But the truth is this manager does not plan ahead; is not really interested in significant organizational results and contributions; does not assess the health and welfare of employees; and is only concerned with what top management believes about the manager's present production level.

Power Manager decisions are made strictly in an incremental manner based on the perception of what the top executive is looking to do next. This manager does not meet with staff to discuss the future direction of the organization. The power manager does what can be done to cut off the flow of upward and downward communication. Employees need to know little more than what they need to get their immediate work done.

Thus, their opinions are to be kept to themselves and information coming from the top executive is not shared with employees unless it is essential to the immediate work performance.

Employees are rarely complimented or encouraged on a daily basis, only told what to do, and as a result they almost never know where they stand and there is little mutual trust and respect between manager and employee. Employees lack enthusiasm and their work products and services lack quality. This is due to the fact that tasks and procedures are basically dictated by the manager, with little opportunity for input and creativity by the employee. Success is based on how closely employees followed procedures or instructions that were provided. While this manager is generally able to maintain an adequate but sufficient level of achievement and production, they are most apt to have low levels of employee satisfaction, and high levels of absenteeism and turnover.

Interpersonal conflict runs high on the staff of the Power Manager. While supervisors are handpicked loyalists, the rest of the staff members are forgotten peons. The interpersonal conflict represents the "tip of the iceberg" of personal conflict that is deeply embedded in the personal frustration of not meeting ones higher level needs. The conflict stems from employees that mirror the manager's lack of concern for others. They initiate conflict by exposing, insulting, or otherwise embarrassing other employees that they view as non-productive, or falling below par for performance. The

Power Manager resolves personnel conflicts by moving people away from the source of conflict. Thus intolerant team leaders, for example, do not learn but rather become stubborn and inflexible in their style and ineffective in motivating employees.

Once an assignment is completed, supervisors and team leaders working for the Power Manager must wait for their next assignment before marching onward with what they believe is the next most important task to tackle. Only the Power Manager can initiate, direct and control all new actions by the staff. When a work assignment is complete, there is "down time" that must be quietly accepted as part of the job as new assignments will be forthcoming only on the manager's discretion. Self initiated projects are viewed as unacceptable diversions of energy that may interfere with the next assignment.

Power Managers never admit being wrong. That is, there is never a situation that is clearly their fault. In such a case where they are entirely to blame, they will apologize profusely, but somehow while citing intentions and actions they took, they will twist and turn, and find a way to indict someone else or compare their actions against others who did much worse, and always seek a way to evade blame or the severity of penalty.

Employees' Manager

The Employees' Manager cares about organizational improvement, productivity, and cost-effectiveness. They try to recruit the best and the brightest employees so they can make the greatest contributions. These managers are considered Employees' Managers because they engage their employees in all aspects of the work, they determine quickly and insightfully how they and their staff can make a difference, and they bring out the best in every employee.

To all employees, the Employees' Manager above all conveys the message that they care about them as people even more than they care how much they know or their raw ability. Given any set of employees, this manager is confident that they can inspire top performance in all, make them better workers than they have ever been and secure them and their organizational unit a better future. They find creative ways to match talent with need, fitting employees to the appropriate jobs, and consistently exceed top management's expectation for performance.

This Manager is characterized by their originality and innovation, their ability to analyze many perspectives quickly, and for developing creative new ideas for improving the organization. They gain synergy through staff input and quickly are able to gain group consensus through a participatory manner, when desirable. This manager trusts employees to do the right thing and does not need to know every step in the process. As a result, supervisors and team leaders feel more autonomous, while their manager has more freedom of mind to explore new avenues for further improvement and development.

The Employees' Manager focuses on the advancement

of the organization, and in the process raises the pride and morale of staff with each achievement. The direction, spirit, and effort of this manager translate into the growth, achievement, and satisfaction of employees. This manager knows how to do the work they are motivating others to do, and can work alongside them, or adjust their management style or approach according to the needs of the individual and task assignment. Their style is "directive" where there is a need to precisely tell who needs to do what, by when, or where complete knowledge is known ahead. Their style is "participatory" when the choices are many and ill-defined, when there is time for staff involvement, or when there is need to explore the cost/benefits of alternatives.

The participatory style is viewed by this manager as a valuable method for gaining needed information and engaging employees in the policy, planning, performance, and evaluation process. The employees' manager may often look like a coach, cheerleader, advisor, or advice seeker, rather than a boss. The staff understands, trusts, and responds in the most appropriate and effective manner. They know the manager is not moved by self-interest alone, but through a greater commitment to both organization and employee.

Employees' Managers make decisions that are much more creative, rational, and refined than could have been developed without full and open employee input. This manager gets the most out of each employee, and employee's sense fairness and parity in work distribution. Employees like their work and work situation and they are aware of their importance to the organization. These managers share information with all staff so every employee knows where the organization is heading and how their efforts contribute. Employees work hard willingly, genuinely appreciate their manager, and trust that their work will be recognized and rewarded. They also know that their manager, when appropriate, will not only offer direct praise to the employee but will frequently do so in front of their peers and the top executive. The manager always gives credit for a job well done, and acknowledges the source of good ideas and product improvement efforts.

This Manager does not hold back aspiring leaders, rather gives them challenges and opportunities for growth. All staff are given chances to share their expertise and ideas with the top executive so the ideas become known and those employees regarded and rewarded for making unique and significant contributions. This manager promotes ideas, does not prevent them, and this is why they are filled with vision. They are the best ones to lead the organization when there is environmental uncertainty or complex technological decisions to be made. They generally are highly analytical and strive to determine and carefully weigh cost-effectiveness in short and long range plans and decisions.

The Employees' Manager is always looking to make a contribution to people's lives as well as serve the organization. They try to set a climate for employee success, the kind of place people want to work, not because of the physical surroundings but due to the spirit that pervades the employees, their sense of purpose and fulfillment, fairness and morale. Employees not only accomplish great things, but they have fun doing it. Employees work together, help one another through heavy workloads, and genuinely care for each other. Management control is minimized and performance maximized. Reasonable risk taking and innovation are encouraged; being the best is the goal.

This Manager thinks of ways to develop and fully utilize employees. They think of ways to stimulate and unblock those that are frustrated or relieve those under undue stress. They try to create an environment of open communication where conflict can easily be voiced and leads to improvement and healthy alternatives, not dysfunctional outcomes. Employees are extremely productive because their work and enthusiasm is focused, aggressive and diversionary responses to the stress and strain of the job are minimized. The climate meets employee needs for mutual respect.

As much as possible within the workplace, this Manager looks for the truth, works for justice, and provides freedom needed by employees. They take the "morally correct" though not always "politically-correct" position even when it may compromise their own security and status within the organization. The Employees' Manager never tries to look good at the expense of others, nor tries to receive unfair advantage or gain favor in a less than meritorious manner. This Manager has a long list of employees from other staffs that want to join up whenever there are openings. Their staff is characterized by their low absenteeism and turnover, and by their high satisfaction and enthusiasm, and by an overall sense of fulfillment from their working experience. The Employees' Manager is the best example of a leader and the closest example of a manager that applies the Judeo-Christian principles to the work setting.

The Marginal Manager

The Marginal Manager is completely ineffective as a leader. This manager is concerned only with maintaining "adequate" productivity or services, and does not care to "risk" changes needed to potentially improve organizational cost-effectiveness. This manager places no emphasis on excellence and little real concern and attention about meeting high work standards. To improve the work process or restructure staff to enhance performance is believed to be too difficult or disruptive.

The Marginal Manager is only going through the motions and is otherwise as withdrawn as is possible from work issues. This manager relies on others to get the work done and only makes any effort to be responsive when there is the need to keep the workers from forming a cabal and mutinying. In any case, this Manager fails to meet the true needs of the organization and his/her employees.

The Marginal manager is either too socially "attached or detached" to their employees, that is, is needy and forms cliques, or is apathetic and stays away from staff interaction, or in another regard, strays away to other diversions, such as drugs, alcohol, or personal pleasures. The three types of Marginal Managers, then, include the:

- Socially-Needy Manager;
- Non-Participant Observer Manager; or
- Diversion-Addicted Manager.

The *"Socially Needy Manager"* is highly deficient in helping the organization because they are too busy struggling to meet their own social approval and esteem needs. Their nature is usually loud, obnoxious, patronizing and back slapping. They typically go through exaggerated motions and histrionics in the effort of performing their normal daily duties. They know what everyone is doing because their "favorites" hang out with the Manager in his/her office which is the grand central station of gossip, the warehouse for unearthing past skeletal remains, and the clearinghouse for rumor. The rest of the staff keep their nose to the grindstone and plug along to get the job done, so the organizational unit can at least get the basic minimum accomplished to save their jobs.

The *"Non-Participant Observer Manager"* has withdrawn because of both social disapproval and the lack of self-actualization fulfillment. They become recluse, timid and reticent out of frustration from not being included in upper management decision making or the serious work of the organization. It is often not due to their personality or ability, but is usually the result of office politics and injustice. That is, these Managers may have been an Employees' Manager at one time, but were unjustly denied promotion or overlooked due to political correctness, and were unfairly transferred from a position of power and influence to a position of little regard. Their reassignment may have been out of jealously for their success which became a threat to a Power Manager. They are stuck in a position that perhaps is located in an unfavorable program in which they have no background experience, education, or interest. This Manager may also report to a Power Manager whose only wish is to expedite this manager's retirement. They do this by controlling all staff activities for which the Marginal Manager is responsible for, undermining their authority and making every effort to render the manager impotent. This manager will often shrink inwardly from the lack of personal fulfillment and achievement which will cause overwhelming depression and mental health issues.

The *"Diversion-Addicted Manager* looks for outlets to escape the frustration and embarrassment of being marginalized. This Manager is often a Non-Participant Observer Manager that has taken a slide downward through a loss in moral fortitude. This individual will find an outlet for their frustration through social affiliations at work (that leads to extramarital affairs), or finds other diversions (abuse of travel, sick leave, pornography, alcohol or drugs).

Developing the Employees' Manager

There are many instruments that compare managers according to their personality, management style, or temperament. The assumption is that managers function differently according to each, and employees should consider what match to each is most favorable for one's own personality, temperament or even gender. While all of this makes some sense, and while managers certainly have a wide range of personalities and style, what makes for an effective manager is the same in any type of organization or line of work. It is simply the character of the manager. As defined previously, only the character of the Employees' Manager is one worth emulating.

The Employees' Manager may not always rise to become the top choice in the selection process or Manager Pool but it is because they are always a threat to Power Managers. They however are the most likely to succeed in having a genuine moral impact on the people that work for them, and the superiors and peers who interact with them. Under their leadership, the organization will have its best chance for success and its greatest advancement in cost-effective operations.

What determines a manager's character are things such as the degree of concern for the organization as well as employees and peers; the openness to ideas flowing from employees; the acceptance of criticism and response to conflict; the handling of information, rewards, and credit (how each is received, given, and shared); the degree of controls on the staff; and the balance of staff work and degree of fulfillment from work.

The Marginal Manager may have ability and sometimes show concern for their employees; they lack sustained motivation, vision, and productivity. The Power Manager may be sufficiently strong in ability and achievement but are often short-sighted in what is good for the organization, entirely deficient in the human relations areas since they are only interested in self-promotion.

In regards to Maslow's hierarchy of needs, while the Marginal Manager (Socially-Needy) may meet many social needs for some of their employees (but not the large majority of staff), they entirely avoid the challenge of self-actualization, being all one can be, and helping others be all they can be. The Power Manager with the "me-first" attitude may be reacting to a genuine fear for their own survival, safety, and security at the workplace, which may be the result of a past failure in the human relations or self-esteem areas. They develop a dysfunctional distrust and aggressive reaction toward all in the workplace. The Marginal Manager (Diversion-Addicted) "runs away" from stress; the Power Manager "fights away." Both reactions are behaviorally learned responses (the primitive instincts of "flight or fight") that have become deeply ingrained into the personality and are manifested as a result of the workplace, or are brought into the workplace from difficulties coping with outside pressures.

The Employees' Manager knows how to give employees freedom on the job for self-expression and a chance to make their own self-generated contributions. They also are able to cut employees loose quickly who find other jobs, giving them a chance for further promotion and self-development, and then quickly fill behind with other high quality candidates waiting in the wings for a chance to work on their staff. The Power Manager and the Marginal Manager do not want to hear or see the development of employee self expression, conflict, or new ideas. Each is viewed as difficult to control or causes too much commotion. Both managers also have a difficult time letting go of employees and take whatever action under their authority to make their employees' departure difficult, uncertain, or delayed. Neither manager has an easy time finding or recruiting quality replacements.

It is not easy to recruit the Employees' Manager and it may take years of work to develop one from within the organization. To hasten the learning process often produces negative results as the individual may become overwhelmed and out of a fear of failure exhibit a regressive behavior like the Marginal Manager or aggressive and controlling behavior like the Power Manager.

Since hiring from the outside is the greater risk, finding and developing leaders from within, seems a better strategy. This effort includes providing training on the different manager types, and on Maslow's motivational theory, and then to undertake periodic assessments including self examinations that can help a new manager stride toward becoming an effective Employees' Manager. The process is first to recognize employees that demonstrate certain leadership abilities, and then develop them through training and on-the-job experiences over several years.

Manager Decision Making and Employee Relations

The Power Manager uses an aggressive style and the legitimate power of position (i.e., selective use of coercion, fear, and rewards) to maintain both control of decision making and the production of goods or services, at the expense of employee intellectual involvement and trust. Employees are valued only as far as getting done the immediate work at hand. From these managers, there is little or no thanks given employees, just a handing out of the next task. These managers live and feel good only to serve themselves and their superior.

The Employees' Managers resist temptations to respond in aggressive and diversionary manners when stress is great, frustrations run high, or needs are not being met. They are firm but proper toward other managers and employees that exude aggressive and diversionary behaviors, and politely prod them toward more appropriate responses, stressing the positive in them. This Manager looks for and sees the great value of every individual, and adds value to them by promoting their strengths, providing them tasks where they can excel, and selecting them for positions where they can be outstanding.

The Power Manager does not give all employees equal benefit of the doubt. Their perception of the value of employees is based on the relative worth of their ability to the tasks at hand currently in demand. The Power

Manager controls all operations and keeps all credit to oneself, except that which is orchestrated for an ulterior purpose. Blame for things gone wrong can never be attached to this manager; always it is a subordinate that did not do what they were told. This manager cannot take the slightest objection let alone criticism from employees. It is quickly viewed as conflict and is deemed offensive and threatening.

The Employees' Manager however, does not look inward as the source of all good and ability to control destiny but rather acknowledges that it is others and God's influence in the work process keeping everything going. He gives credit where appropriate, and particularly to the employees that are doing the work. There is nothing concealed or orchestrated to divert attention from truth or to control credit. When something goes wrong this manager steps in to accept responsibility and protects employees. Feedback on employee concerns and interests toward assignments is encouraged.

The Power Manager is not interested in cueing employees in on what is happening, exploring the truth in issues and problems, building staff unity, balancing work, or correcting staff problems. This manager tends to elicit three types of employee responses that are "highly toady, antagonistic, or apathetic." The Power Manager is interested only in the top priorities of the moment getting done to gain immediate attention and reward from their superior. When there are work problems and staff conflicts and issues, they are resolved quickly by reassigning staff to get the immediate work done, and repositioning or removing those that are quickly perceived as the source of the problem. Employees learn to comply with managers' demands without question (toady response). These employees come into favor with the manager and are promoted into supervisory positions on the assumption of continuing a blind loyalty to the leader. They become oblivious to their former peers, some of whom they now supervise. The larger portion of the staff have an adverse reaction either resenting the toady behavior or are desensitized to it, and just feel a tremendous emptiness, a void of true relations. These employees become antagonistic, disgruntled, or apathetic, and split away from the loyalists, causing a major cleft between staff, and with manager and staff relations in general.

In comparison, the Employees' Manager tends to promote fairness, honesty, and good will among employees. This manager is interested in getting to the truth of matters and resolving issues wisely and justly. They seek to keep staff informed and involved, knowledgeable of each other's work and what is happening around the organization, maintaining a balanced work distribution, and building staff unity. They listen and communicate openly with staff on needs, interests, concerns and problems. These managers look for the best in everyone and employees respond with their best. These managers ensure that relations are good with all employees and in their relationship to all employees.

To the Power Manager, employees' "failure to use good

judgment" means they did not listen well enough to what they were told to do. Employees come under great stress if they are not sure exactly what the manager wanted and fail to ask for clarification. Employees own best judgment is never enough for this manager, things must be done the manager's way down to the minutest degree. The Power Managers want competent but nameless bag carriers who meet with their manager only to find out what their next assignment will be.

The Power Managers' tolerance is thin and their ability to forgive minimal. Their employees become oversensitive, carrying with them a distrusting, threatening, and lingering sense of fear of potential reprisal or even banishment. These managers are known to have employees repositioned into the "penalty box" (someone given little to do and is forced to watch others get good assignments, make contributions, and get ahead); put into "solitary confinement" (someone given a position of no responsibility with an office like the janitor's closet); banished to the farthest outpost (someone moved to a physical location that is the least desirable duty station in the organization); or, put on permanent detail (moving from one meaningless extended assignment to another, whichever is least attractive).

The mental and physical abuse of employees resulting from these "repositioning" schemes are all to the personal delight of the Power Manager, reflections of their power. Each option is enjoyed by the manager according to the length of time it effectively removes the employee from the mainstream of work and from having any contact with the Power Manager. The only thing that brings such an employee back into good relations with the Power Manager is if the employee somehow comes into good graces with the Power Manager's superior. Then, the self-centered Power Manager actively seeks an entirely new relationship with the employee; one that ignores the past, and never asks for forgiveness, but rather only focuses on the present.

In comparison, the Employees' Manager trusts their employees to make the right decision and forgives their mistakes. They have empowered their employees. Relations are genuine, trusting, productive, and rewarding. The manager and employees nourish and enrich one another like a functional family. Employee experiences from a dysfunctional past (e.g., wounds from working under the other two types of managers) are healed and the individual is made whole and optimally functions again, with restored self-worth. These managers do not categorize some employees as "problem employees" to be identified and shipped off. They can handle their share of "problem employees" without sending them off to unenviable duty-stations; they address matters and correct them, if at all humanly possible. They make every attempt to do the right thing for the individual and long term good of the organization.

The Marginal Manager only proceeds with what they are told to do and expects employees to proceed only with what they are told to do. The bottom line is "not to rock the boat." They depend on operating in their own comfort zone and are comfortable only with the status quo. In contrast, the Power Manager has a personal stake in getting ahead and is always posturing for the best vantage point to proceed with such a plan. In this respect, the Power Manager is always in aggressive pursuit of immediate payoff projects. Although difficult, technical or long range issues are largely ignored, at least the Power Manager produces well on short term projects. The problem for the organization is that both the Marginal and Power Managers prove disastrous in making difficult decisions that affect the long term health of the organization.

Employees working for the Power Manager are always concerned about appearances such as how they look, how their products look (conforming to a standard format), how their ambition is perceived (coming in early, staying late), how their intelligence is perceived (quick recall from rote memorization of numbers or things that could have been easily found in reference documents), etc. Employees generally know not to ask for flexibility in work, work setting, or work scheduling. Employees are always weary that the manager is looking for their weaknesses or their moment of indiscretion, or the seldom mistake that they might make. The focus is on what a person cannot do and how they relate to the manager, rather than what they could contribute to the good of the organization.

In comparison, appearances are not important to the Employees Manager; rather substance, merit, and contribution are important. This manager is not as concerned about control as in performance; they trust their employees and are very flexible within reason to variation in work, work setting, and scheduling.

The Employees' Manager depend on the judgment of employees to know when to look good, how to act, but most importantly when and how to perform. Employees know that their manager is looking to use their strengths for an important organizational contribution. They find employee strengths and optimize them for performance not conformance, empowering common employees to make uncommon achievement. These managers issue challenging demands more often from the suggestions of employees, not commands narrowly conceived and directed. The Employees' Manager wants performers, not pleasers.

The Power Manager checks on conformance and repeatedly calls attention to the errors made by others. The Employees Manager is not a checker but is a doer; they identify all aspects of the problem and work to correct the deeper-set system problems that cause the reoccurrence of the problems. The Power Manager works on a single track on problems, while the Employees' Manager works on multiple tracks to get to the source of issues and find efficient long term solutions. In the technology area, for example, the Power Manager spends two years buying equipment, two years setting up a network and then begins plans to develop software, which by its completion will need new computers. The Employees' Manager is working on improving existing software and upgrading to improved databases simultaneously while purchasing equipment and networks that take full advantage of technology, keeping his staff involved in programming and maintenance of systems, and putting the organization in a better position to more effectively manage the present and address the future.

Developing Organizational Strength through Effective Management

Organizational strength is developed when managers strive to meet organizational goals and employee needs at the highest capacity; only when managers strive to be "Employees' Managers" can an organization reach its highest potential.

The number one priority for organizations, the top priority of the TOP model, is to develop strong leadership. In order to become a most effective manager, it is essential to understand the business of management, employee motivation and performance, and manager character. Striving to attain the fundamental principles of management is critical to the quest for organizational strength. To be a most cost-effective organization, all managers within an organization must work together to attain the greatest organizational strength, and this requires the application of the following basic understandings:

1. Effective management can be learned and all personality styles can become effective managers

if they strive strongly toward the good of the organization and employees at the same time. Management effectiveness is not so much based on intelligence, imagination, and knowledge as it is on the motivation to be an effective manager.

2. For the right manager to be selected for a position, there must be a sense of truth, justice, and freedom about the candidate. Truth, in that one really cares for and feels called to the position; justice, in that it was acquired based on merit and fairness; and freedom, in that it was a voluntarily act to take the job and was not the result of heavy handed pressure for some expedient or selfish motive. Self actualization and fulfillment of organization and employee needs will be enhanced the more these conditions are met.

3. When managers ignore organizational concerns and employees needs and strengths in the determination of job tasking, a great deal of employee frustration and displacement of energy occurs. When employees path to contributing to the organization is blocked and their needs are unfulfilled, patterns of dysfunctional behavior prevail which tend to be aggressive or diversionary in nature.

4. The best managers excel at keeping the staff highly motivated and equally engaged in meaningful work that will eventually make a

significant contribution to the organization. Their methods improve productivity, challenge the intellect, and promote high quality performance and morale. This manager is successful because they seek to optimize the fulfillment of organizational goals and the full range of needs of employees (including survival/safety, social approval/esteem, and self-actualization).

5. In order to be at least minimally effective as a manager, one must continuously review and improve their planning, organizing, and controlling abilities (as previously defined), and sharpen staff skills in the diagnostic, administrative, and technical areas. The more defined and urgent the task, the more directive the manager is able to be. Ever conscious to boredom intrinsic in some work processes, however, the effective manager seeks every means to engage employees in process improvement efforts.

6. To every situation, meeting, and interaction, vertically and horizontally, within and outside the organization, the effective manager strives to add something to improve the situation, uncover the solution, or fulfill individual or group needs. This manager assesses one's own efforts and those of the staff and finds their "value-added" contribution in an idea or an effort. That is, effective managers strive to bring out the

leadership ability of all individuals, superiors and subordinates in which they interact. They see the best in all people, find their strengths, and are able to draw it out for their own good and the good of the organization.

7. Effective managers track their staff's progress toward making significant organizational contributions. They assess the organization's strength, use questionnaires and random interviews to evaluate staff climate, and seek staff input to improve areas most in need of change. These may involve changes within one's self, one's group, the relations between staff, as well as relations with others on the horizontal and vertical dimensions of the organization.

8. The higher an employee's intelligence, ability, and experience with task demands, the less the employee will accept concrete directives, and in particular in those areas lacking certainty of what might be the most appropriate means and ends. Likewise, the more a manager can successfully interpret and respond to environmental demands directly and independently of superiors, the more fulfilled and supportive are employees.

9. No amount of self-confidence, charisma, expertise, or intelligence of the manager can overcome the opposite thwarting force of one's superior who is bound to control their actions. The power within any position and its

corresponding responsibility is always determined by one's superior. The longer an effective manager is boxed into a tightly controlled position with little ability to act on initiatives and innovations, the greater is the detriment to the organization, the individual, and their subordinate staff. The Power Manager tends to absorb the subordinate manager's authority by controlling such things as employee recruiting, promoting, reassignment of subordinates, and decision making discretion for anything but the most minor day-to-day functions. Thus, any prospective manager needs to weigh these considerations carefully prior to accepting a job offer from a Power Manager.

10. Becoming an effective manager means being the kind of leader that always looks for ways to move the organization to be more cost-effective, to develop employees to be more productive and fulfilled, and to grow oneself into a person with stronger moral character. An effective manager will use the ten organizational priorities (TOP model) to continuously improve the organization.

Chapter 6

Employees: Being the Best

As identified in the previous chapter, the knowledge, attitude and behavior of the manager directly affects the work environment, the manager-employee relationships, and the behavior and productivity of employees. The employee is sensitive to their manager's verbal and non-verbal expressions, to what they say and do, and what they fail to say and do.

Some employees have never worked for a manager that they really cared to work for and thus, have never had an opportunity to become the type of employee they are capable of being. In the process, they may have developed bad work habits and lowered the perception of themselves and their abilities. This deprived sense of self diminishes their performance and sense of personal fulfillment.

When faced with a difficult work environment, it is the duty of the employee to assess their situation and assertively work to correct it, or to move into another work situation where they can start anew. There, with another manager, there is hope they can bring forward their best self and best work performance possible. Everyone must assess if their job is a good fit for them, but once reasonably accepting that it is, then it is every employee's daily challenge to be the best they can be.

The reasons why an employee wants to work for a certain type of manager are much the same as why a manager wants to have certain types of employees work for them. Just as there are "Employees' Managers", there is a type of employee that every manager would love to have. This employee might be called, "Every Manager's Employee." The Every Manager's Employee has concern for doing their best work always as well as concern for their manager and follow employees.

The Managers' Employee has certain characteristics that make them great workers and tremendous people. These "dream" employees are the type of person a manager both respects and admires for the work they do and the people they are. The Managers' Employee is the type of person that is a joy to work with, and is one whom the manager has no problems, anxieties, or concerns about promoting.

The Manager's Employee is not a "yes man." They are not aggressive and pushy or withdrawn and submissive, and do not reflect the mannerisms of the Power Managers or Marginal Managers. Rather, this employee is "assertive" in the way that they bring the right attitude and response to every situation; consistently creating win-win effects.

 It does not matter if one works for the Power Manager, the Marginal Manager, or the Employees' Manager everyone can do better if they know how to approach each situation assertively. Assertive employees know what drives their bosses. Manager types differ according to how much they care about the organization, their responsibility, and their employees. While the Employees' Manager will ensure employees are assertive and do their best, the employee must strive more earnestly to find a successful way to be assertive with the other two types of managers. This is particularly important not only for one's own health, but for one's career retention and advancement.

There are real challenges to overcome in order to become Every Manager's Employee. In some cases, the challenge is the Manager's style; in other cases, the employee lacks the right attitude or social graces; and others may just be improperly prepared for the work at hand. The challenge that confronts each employee is to assess where one currently stands in terms of their attitude, ability, and eagerness to perform their job. The Manager's Employee is always trying to do their best and always striving to do even better.

Types of Employees

The following describes three types of employees:

- The **"Go-Getter"** is the typical "Every Manager's Employee." They are totally engaged in their work, giving their best for whatever is needed. These individuals are not just energized new employees, but come to work every day with great vitality. These are competent eager-to-learn employees who love their jobs and are good toward the other people at work. They often have experienced worse jobs or know people who work in worse situations; they are humble and grateful for their jobs. They may know others who have a worse boss and work for less pay, or may lack the qualifications and experience of others on the same job and feel they need to work harder to prove themselves. They may see their situation as a once in a lifetime opportunity or one that could led to a great new opportunities and career advancement. The go-getter is highly motivated with and possesses a genuine desire to contribute and do meaningful work.

- The **"Steady Freddie"** is one partially engaged in their work, but who often need some help or stimulation to finish work in an excellent manner. These individuals may be stuck in grade, not motivated by money or career advancement potential, or may be distracted by self interests outside the job, such as a relationship, a hobby, or other consuming interests. The steady Freddie gives a decent day's work effort but usually has something else going on in their life that is creating friction and drawing down their attitude and performance on the job.

- The **"Unplugged"** is one who has become disengaged as evidenced in their cynical or apathetic attitude and performance. They most likely have been left behind and overlooked by managers and by their peers who have advanced, or have been placed in embarrassing situations where they are passed over for important assignments. These employees may need resuscitation or a jump start; healing or counseling; personal space or a "2 by 4" to the backside; or need to be repositioned in the organization or be fired or given the option to resign. The unplugged often needs help getting the job done right. They have a difficult time sustaining any level of high performance. They get stuck in their position because they are stigmatized, and thus become immoveable within the organization because their reputation precedes them.

The go-getter is doing all the right things and looking for ways to improve. The steady Freddie is okay as is but needs a gentle push to improve. The unplugged needs more than a little help to get going again. Each type can be helped with an understanding of what is expected from an ideal employee, and what one to improve from their current state, particularly when facing small, medium and large difficulties at work.

Ideal Employee Characteristics

The characteristics of an Every Manager's Employee:

1. **Producer.** The manager looks for people who do outstanding work and can never seem to get enough work to do. These employees are not fussy about the type of work they receive and do a good job with anything given. When completed, their product needs little or no change and they ask for more work or otherwise help others with their work.

2. **Committed.** Every manager wants to have people that have a genuine interest and commitment to help carry forward the vision that they have for the organization.

An employee who has similar drive, interest, and motivation as the manager, and adds value to his/her vision, will be successful.

3. **Planner.** This trait is epitomized in the worker who is always looking ahead to what might need to get done. They have a pulse on what is happening within and outside of the organizational environment and they strive to assess the impact. This individual is indispensable to the manager because they are often a step ahead of the manager who may frequently be too busy or too close to the action of the office or operation.

4. **Organizer.** This worker is very organized and keeps everyone on track. A smart manager will use these skills to shape up the office and to help others learn how to be better organized and accountable. This employee is supported by all if they share their skills in a manner that is supportive of the staff, helping them to do better, as well as potentially gain income, promotion, or recognition.

5. **Challenger.** A good manager deeply appreciates those dedicated few who think of all aspects of plans and can refine or offer suggestions for challenging alternative plans that would be more cost-effective. A well thought-out alternative to an existing policy, plan, or action that will improve the organization, the organizational unit, or staff is always welcome. If an employee does not like what management is doing, they first need to collect sufficient information to understand somewhat thoroughly the manager's position and then come

forward and raise the matter in a sensitive way for discussion in private with the manager.

6. **Loyal.** Every manager looks for indications that the employee can be trusted on a personal as well as professional level. This loyalty must be based on mutual respect for the manager as a person as well as confidence in their ability, judgment, and leadership qualities. This type of loyalty is not based on a selfish desire for advancement or gaining inside influence, but for the good of the organization and the welfare of the manager within the organization. The employee should be able to speak directly and honestly to the manager in a friendly nature, but not show blind loyalty to a superior nor act from a selfish motive.

7. **Learner.** Whenever there is a need for more knowledge on the staff, where there is something that needs to be learned to achieve organizational goals, this individual is willing to volunteer to learn it. This individual will be glad to accept hours or cost to support the learning but will also volunteer their own time and money, within reason, to learn and better accomplish the organizational goals. This worker is always trying to do the job better and are either strengthening their own skills or experimenting with ways to speed up work processes and improve productivity.

8. **Enthusiastic.** Every manager looks for employees who want to maximize organizational accomplishment and have fun in the process, and the natural ingredients that one looks for is enthusiasm, creativity, and good natured

regard for others.

9. **Perspective.** Every manager needs employees who track with them on the importance of work tasks, particularly when there are high priorities that require enormous energy, focus, and teamwork to accomplish. Perspective involves attentiveness to current needs and demands, and awareness of priorities, and of their history and background. Employees cannot be expected to gain perspective instantly, but good employees will acquire it from extra research. They will even come to understand a manager's non-verbal cues and quick reactions that stem from past experiences and relate to the unstated meaning behind decisions and actions.

10. **Humorous.** As part of the individual and collective psyche, it is critical that after every important effort or task accomplishment and at certain points throughout, there is a need for healthy emotional release. Individuals with a good sense of humor or those who know what to say and do to break the intensity, and as a result, will serve the greater good by helping to make people feel relaxed, relieved, happy, and glad to be a part of the work team.

Transitions and Work Environment Challenges

Becoming the type of employee that has many, most, or all of the traits described above for the ideal employee requires continuous work on both an intrapersonal and interpersonal level. On an intrapersonal account, much of who we are at work is transference of who we are outside of work. If we are happy with ourselves and our situation outside of work, most of us can endure the worst of situations at work. The workplace is a wonderful place for the expression of who we are but is still, however, no substitute for the fulfillment of the complete person that we are called to be. Often, it is the person that has created much of their own identity around the work place that becomes devastated whenever there is anything resembling a threatening type of situation at work (e.g., a reorganization) or if anything goes wrong at work (e.g., miss an important deadline). This is when it dawns on the individual that there needs to be a life beyond the workplace.

Nevertheless, work is very important financially, socially, and psychologically, and consumes a large part of one's time and space in life. It is essential to do all one can to make the work experience a positive experience. Moreover, work is supposed to be personally rewarding and fulfilling, and hopefully be making some small contribution to the betterment of the world.

Within any business or government job, employees might encounter a work environment that is less than fulfilling whenever there are problems with one's own manager or in the manager ranks. This is common when one's manager is a Power Manager or a Marginal Manager who perceive employees worth as objects for their own purpose or survival. Both operate on the basis of the task at hand; neither truly caring for their employees nor having much interest in the true welfare of the organization.

Many problems can arise from the work environment when there is a transition at the top that can negatively affect employees, including the:

- often contrary values and agendas of new top managers or political appointees as opposed to previous top managers, and the corresponding policy shifts that occur;

- need to deal with the lack of enthusiasm from hardened veteran middle-managers who have become disenfranchised and disinterested because of being unjustly passed over for a higher position, or who have trained one too many new managers who have now surpassed them (the Marginal Manager);

- employees being caught in the middle of on-going ill-spiritedness from unresolved personal vendettas between certain managers who have offended one another during past power struggles (the Power Manager(s));

- unexpected shift in approach from new and impressionable top managers or political appointees, who lack understanding of the business operation and often become influenced most by whomever speaks to them last (the rash new manager); and,

- new top managers who mistakenly promote the individual that seeks selfish recognition and advancement by going outside of their chain-of-command to make a quick positive impressions (the naïve new manager).

When there is a new top manager, the transition process can produce much abuse. Under such circumstances, the challenge to become or sustain being an Every Managers' Employee is enormous. These issues diminish ones energy, enthusiasm, and motivation. Thus, managers must constantly seek to be Employees' Managers and motivate employees if they are to retain the employees they desire.

Regardless of the transition at the top, one's immediate manager sets the environment for their employees. The Employee's Manager helps the situation naturally by their handling of the situation. Power Managers and Marginal Managers can do the same by trusting more in their employees and letting go, loosening control over work process, governing not ruling over employees, inviting staff feedback and friendly relations, increasing employees' freedom of expression, and taking risks that might payoff for the good of the organization and employees. The problem is that during times of transition, they tighten the controls.

Power Managers and Marginal Managers laden the organization with many employee problems, intensify whatever negative organizational impacts are being felt by all employees and tend to negate whatever zeal the employees may have had for the new changes at the top. Under such management, open communication and trust is endangered, and the manager rarely gets the truth from employees. Instead, employees' true thoughts and feelings are spoken only within the narrow confines of trusted comrades on strictly confidential terms. The general staff communication becomes superficial as employees feel disconnected or subservient, and generally want to avoid communication with each other. They do not want to risk saying something openly such as a critical or cynical comment that they will regret later.

In general, Employees' Managers help to develop their employees into "Go-Getters" or "Every Managers' Employees;" the Power Manager tends to produce the "Steady Freddy's;" and the Marginal Manager tends to generate the "Unplugged." This generalization of course does not hold firm because each individual has the power to rise above their situation and environmental constraints. For this to occur, however, employees must be able to assess the situation they are in and develop their own strategy to achieve the highest level of employee effectiveness in spite of the constraints set by the character of their manager.

Problems of employee motivation and performance typically go under the radar of the Power and Marginal Managers, and when they are acknowledged, these managers will rarely ever come to realize that their own character as a manager is the primary reason for the problems exhibited by their employees. When employees' needs and hopes are ignored by management, instead of an honest open discussion of issues, conflicts and tensions, a siege mentality among employees persists. It exists not only between management and staff but between staff, as one cannot risk trusting another.

Employees develop a subculture for communicating by argot. They go through the motion of friendly open hallway banter with each other only to acknowledge a mutual agreement on the fatalistic nature of the environment without saying anything directly. For example, the typical elevator conversation might begin with a loaded question that has a deeper meaning that reflects a sense of disillusionment:

- "What time of the day is it?" (i.e., how long do we have until close of business?);

- "What day of the week is it?" (i.e., how long until it is time to go home for the weekend?);

- "How much longer do you have?" (i.e., how many years, months, days, and sometimes hours are left until one's own retirement?), and/or,

- "How much longer do we have?" (i.e., how long is it to the boss's retirement or to a new Administration and top manager?).

Employees should never simply resign themselves to a situation that clearly is hopeless because they may be in for a long wait for change. Employees, who find themselves on a staff where honest communication and feelings are stifled, quickly come to a dilemma. They must decide to address the issues with the manager or become resign to the fact that they will never become the best they can be on that staff. If they are willing to take the risk to make their thoughts known to the manager, it is important to understand that the manager may respond in any of the following possible ways:

- Accept them and the suggested change and respect the employee for the input (a reforming Power or Marginal Manager);

- View it as criticism and take some action immediately against the employee for raising the issues or do so at a later date on some unrelated issue (Power Manager);

- Say little or nothing and do little or nothing, or promise to do something but do nothing (Marginal Manager); of

- Do nothing until the time is right and then correct the problem taking full credit for the response (Power Manager).

The task of attempting to change managers and the work environment may seem impossible, but it is not hopeless. To be effective, it is critical for employees to believe that every manager can be made into an Employees' Manager. Employees must look inward to understand the best strategy for improving any situation. Employees have a very different natural response to Power Managers and Marginal Managers, than they do to Employees' Managers. One can only really hope to change what can be changed, but sometimes the seemingly impossible does occur, and managers' attitude and behavior may change as well.

While managers make a huge influence on employee's attitudes and behavior, employees are also affected by office politics, harmful communication, and abusive personalities of other employees. There are innumerable land mines that can make the work experience difficult for the otherwise motivated and competent individual. For employees to feel some sense of satisfaction, they must feel some sense of independence and individual expression on the job. Each step forward in this vein is a step in the right direction and helps employees have a stake in the organization.

It is a special challenge to employees to be the best one can be when their manager makes it very difficult to do so. This can be the case when the employee has an unresolved injustice done them or felt by them, when they may have been unjustifiably downgraded, removed from their position, reassigned without explanation, negatively impacted by a reorganization, or given a low personnel evaluation without justified explanation. The employee is left behind to pick up the pieces and get back to work. It is assumed that despite the on-going embarrassment, affront to ones pride and the constant reminder of the injustice, one is expected to go on as if nothing should be bothering them.

At such points in one's career, an employee needs to take heart and stay in the present. The improvement of organizational and management behavior always begins with improvement of individual's attitude through increased knowledge and changed motives. Individuals that change themselves for the better have the capacity to affect and inspire similar change in others. The converse is true also. Employees with a bad attitude can infect others accordingly or be isolated and ignored by others, but in any case is not a positive influence in the organization.

Unless one is unusually lucky, all employees at some point in their career face some major setback they need to overcome at work. As a result, an employee may shift from being a super charged Go-Getter, to being an unstable Steady Freddie, and if too lax may eventually slide downward to the status of the Unplugged. This is when one's energy and interest level is on empty. On any staff, depending mostly on the character of their manager and past experiences of the staff, employees may vary widely from being very satisfied, engaged, and contributing to the organizational good, to something quite the opposite.

The following are several ideas to keep the "Go-Getter" going, and to energize the "Steady Freddie" and jump-start the "Unplugged." In essence, they are ideas that can help any employee of any type, but may be particularly fitting to each special type based on their unique situation.

Keeping the "Go-Getter" Going

While there is little one ever needs to say to help the "Go-Getter," there are some helpful reminders that even the Go-Getter can always draw some extra motivation, strength and direction from:

1. Respect all. The basic issue for all managers and employees is being able to fulfill their mutual need for respect. Respecting one another starts with self-respect and is completed with respect for others. Receiving the respect of others is out of one's control and needs to be left to others and therefore should not be of any concern or produce worry. If one does a good job with the former, the latter will also occur.

2. When wills agree, the group gets going. To get individuals to a state of agreement, one must find common purpose, and once this is affirmed, there should be little reason to have problems with the manager or one's fellow employees. A common purpose helps individuals work together again and in the process, form renewed relations. Working toward a common purpose overcomes the natural tendency toward self-indulgence and fulfills the need to contribute to a greater cause.

3. Self assess. Identify one's own attitudes and behaviors as being aggressive, inhibited, or assertive. Think through how one might move from aggressive or inhibited to a more assertive attitude and behavior. With assertive attitudes and actions, relive actual situations or simulate future situations. Identify those things that cause the most problems and rank order them. Brainstorm how to address these matters with an assertive outlook.

4. Focus on essential work and work processes. Try to identify areas that need improvement that one might directly help resolve, without sacrificing or diminishing one's own work effort.

5. Get involved. Try to get involved with a group work activity and become an effective team member willing to minimize one's own needs for the sake of the group and the team's tasks.

6. Become more self-sufficient. Try to get through the difficult spots on one's own without draining resources of others or those of the manager. Take time to do homework and draw upon one's own strengths of education, experience, background, and relations to help with any essential workplace task. Search the Internet to find an answer to the problem or difficulty at hand. Cover all bases, do not leave something out thinking that someone else might have that step covered. Complete the entire task with excellence.

7. Become more assertive. Do not remain silent if there is an immediate problem that needs the manager's attention. It is important to raise the issue and speak the truth whether or not anyone else is willing to bring the issue up. Find a way to raise the matter assertively with the only motivation being the good of the organization and employees.

8. Recharge through greater perspective. Find courage and strength in the fact that there is life after work, and one must not evaluate self worth or depend entirely on the workplace for one's highest fulfillment. Work is a means to fulfillment, not complete fulfillment itself. ("We work to live; not live to work.") Find outlets outside of work to recharge batteries and gain better perspective, motivation and performance while at work. Most of all remember that someone of "Go Getter" caliber can almost go anywhere and make an impact, so realize it is good to keep one's eyes open for other options; that there is life after this job.

9. Discard all false pretense and arrogance. Concentrate on how to be a better humble and trusted servant of the manager and one's fellow employees with genuine non-regard for self. One finds real life when willing to submit oneself to the full service of others without the blemish of pride and selfish desire.

10. Search for ways to make a worthy contribution. Look for ways to be an instrument of good to transform the workplace (work and human relations) into something better for the organization and others; something that could not have been without one's involvement.

Energizing the "Steady Freddie"

Energizing the "Steady Freddie" can make the difference needed in transforming a standard or regular employee into an extraordinary and stellar performer, and it can be done just by doing certain little things better:

1. Monitor Priorities. Monitoring priorities involves knowing ones priorities, keeping tasks moving toward accomplishment at an acceptable pace, and avoiding unnecessary involvement with other tasks or individuals that may hinder one's own task progress. Sometimes this means not over-committing to work that one cannot possibly accomplish even through it may be of interest and potentially have be attractive benefits. Other times it may mean limiting ones interactions with certain others so to avoid distraction, interruption, or conflicts with one's own priorities. The unexpected added responsibilities may occur but unless deadlines on priorities can be easily slipped without repercussions, these matters will need to be dealt with within one's own time-line through work efficiencies or unplanned overtime.

2. Clarify Team Assignments. Employees need to clearly understand both the work assignments, as well as how tasks fit into the broader team or organizational goal. In particular, the task result or outcome needs to be defined as well as standards for performance. Each team member needs to understand their roles, responsibilities, and resources that can be assigned to individual and shared tasks. Deadlines for each task and overall project goals and process standards need to be defined upfront.

3. Look for Feedback. When duties and assignments are more open-ended, unclear, and requires more interaction with peers, it is important to get increased feedback from superiors and customers to ensure staying on course. When receiving feedback, listen objectively without interrupting and avoid taking the input as a personal attack (unless it is). Focus on the content, and listen calmly and attentively, there's always a nugget of truth or something to be gained or learned. Feedback should be solicited on concerns that affect the efficiency or quality of the product or service.

4. Give Feedback. Employees often are asked their opinion or are responsible for giving feedback where they see it is necessary. Feedback should begin with a statement of concern about a mutual interest, such as meeting an organizational goal. Focus on the behavior or action, not the person, and talk about the likely impact of continued behaviors and actions on the goal. Then, invite a response and listen carefully. Together decide what to do. Give suggestions, but do not purport to be the expert; instead, leave the individual the flexibility to work out the details of what should be done.

5. Work through Conflicts. Employee conflicts arise from increased pressures to produce; from the stress of producing more within less time or with less resources; from dealing with differences of approach toward a mutual assignment; from the lack of clear enough definition of roles and responsibilities; from clashes due to different backgrounds, personalities or work styles; or even because one's group goals may conflict with those of another group. The best way to overcome conflict is to identify the issue early on and deal with it before it becomes a major problem. If the issue has escalated, focus on the matter, not the emotion, and seek a mutually acceptable resolution. Putting yourself in the others' shoes and express your concerns in a non-threatening manner to gain a mutual understanding.

6. Manage Your Personality. It's easy to get over-stressed or fall into a rut and allow our personality shortcomings or those of others to get the best of us. Some people tend to be dominating, pushy, intimidating, and control communication by talking incessantly (seemingly without breathing). Others avoid issues at all costs, remain silent or expect that problems will disappear on their own or will by simply reciting the higher goals of the organization or waving the flag of quality and customer service. Still others carry emotional baggage and are too willing to recount past problems, events, and grievances. These folks seem to get a nefarious satisfaction with arguments of any kind, engaging in a point-by-point debate and cross-examination of every detail. Avoid the pitfalls of undesirable personality lapses and remember to stay focused on the present task or issue; try to be cool, calm, and collected; and be supportive and empathetic toward others while addressing their concerns.

7. Be In Touch With Emotions. Emotions can help us or ruin us. For every task undertaken and every change in the work environment, there is an emotional response. The emotions are tied to a mixture of underlying feelings, interests, and needs. They are tied to ones sense of self respect and the perception of respect from others. Emotional response can be expected, for example, when one's situation changes through reorganization, budget reductions, accelerated deadlines, tougher competition, new technologies, increased customer demands, etc. The main objective is to use emotions to help, not hinder. As such they must be acknowledged, understood, controlled, and channeled into powerful motivating forces to improve performance, relations, or ones employment experience.

8. Be Determined to Make a Difference. Confucius once said, "It's better to light one candle, than to curse the darkness." Employees may often feel powerless against the machine-like operation of an organization. The truth is that organizations are in constant need of improvement. Be determined to make a difference. Look for work processes that seem redundant or inefficient; a product or service that can be improved; a new technology that is needed; a new task that should be accomplished; a project or change process that is taking too long to implement; a policy that is outmoded; a new market or direction for the organization.

9. Win Support for Your Idea. Suggesting change in organizations often meets quick resistance. People do not want to change their thinking, work habits, position, or relations with others, even if it involves the betterment of the organization. The trick is to translate the idea into both organizational and personal benefits, particularly for those that can be expected to have an immediate adverse reaction. It might be easy to get an idea sold by forcing the issue, but the best approach is to establish a forum for greater employee involvement that will lead to others coming to the same conclusion. These individuals will help you sell the idea and its mutual benefits to others. They may also help to refine the idea or its implementation strategy. The bottom line is to look for ways to involve, not alienate, and to influence, not manipulate others.

10. Understand People's Motivational Buttons. Knowing what motivates others is often essential toward becoming successful. It takes time and experience to know what might motivate certain individuals. Each individual's source of motivation may be slightly different and the more sensitive one is to this feature, the more likely one will be toward achieving their goals. Remember the Maslow principles: people need to achieve, be creative, and satisfy ambition; need to please others and gain recognition, a sense of belonging, and a feeling of being needed; and need a certain level of security and comfort. Employees also need to feel in control of the work and to be fully engaged. This includes being able to apply logic, and analyze data or information to improve workflow and gain control over outcomes. It also means working for the greater good of the organization and the community by improving the quality, quantity, and efficiency of operations. Finally employees want to do all that is feasible to improve their abilities, reduce stress, and enhance job security.

Recharging the "Unplugged"

There is hope for those employees that are not perceived well or are not performing well. The ability and desire to consistently perform at excellent levels requires one to take the following to heart:

1. Count one's blessings. As bad as it seems when one feels detached, disinterested, or depressed, remember that one's situation could be worse, and try to consider how one's present situation could be for the betterment of the person. Do not let go of this thought. Remember that one is still alive and that no matter how bad, humiliating, cruel, or unjust the job seems to be, life could be worse and is for many, particularly for those without a job.

2. Take a fresh look at any new start. Do not jump ship just because of unexpected change or diminishing duties, a difficult personnel evaluation, or some other affront to one's pride. Look upon life's turns as a wonderful learning experience. Find the silver lining in everything. There is life after one has been displaced through reorganization, reassignment, or after one has lost important duties. Often there is less weight on ones shoulders providing more time to think. It may also give one a chance to know people in a refreshing new way whereby one's contacts may be more meaningful and without the pretense and trappings of one's prior influence or status. So reassess the new role from a broad perspective and take encouragement from any new start.

3. Forgive and then redouble the effort. When feeling misused, abused, or falsely accused, one of the hardest things to do is to go along without the "chip on one's shoulder." This is where we must go the extra mile by setting sights on doing one's very best and doing it without an attitude. If one can forgive and not carry the negative attitude, people will respect and admire this, and management will notice it. How a person handles themselves in difficult times can be a very positive character builder. Everyone loves a person who picks himself or herself up off the ground after a fall and gets right back in the race.

4. Keep work and life in balance. Sometimes a work situation can get the best of a person. One may think they are doing everything right and despite one's all-out effort everything turns out wrong. Use this situation as an opportunity for personal reassessment and make sure priorities are in order, with family first. Also, if one lacks interests or hobbies outside of work, find some. Family and interests help put work into perspective, and insure that problems from work will not be so fully occupying and overwhelming. This gives the balance needed to start each day at work fresh and renewed, letting go of the past and focused on the present.

5. Keep reign over negative emotions. When going through any adjustment to a negative work situation, one may feel lonely and depressed as if they are the only ones this has ever happened to. Realize that such negative things happen to everybody at some time in their career. At the time, it may feel like a terminal illness but it is not, and one can recover fully and the experience will greatly add to one's ability to relate to others who have had similar experiences.

6. Don't burn the bridge. If you choose to go take a new job at another organization, do not shake the dust off your shoes as you leave, but remember to be gracious to all who have given you their support over the years, and even those who have not. Remember some of the best jobs are those that one leaves and then comes back to after certain things have changed, one's spirit is renewed, experience enriched, and a new opportunity suddenly avails itself.

7. Look at prospects realistically. Before deciding to go to a new job, remember that there will always be "problematic" and strange personalities wherever one goes. The grass is not always greener on the other side. One must adjust to new work, new people, and a new work environment all at once. As the saying goes, "sometimes the devil you know is better than the devil you don't know." Think all this through rationally rather than emotionally before making a decision you might regret.

8. Fight the temptation not to care. No amount of knowledge, experience, or ability, nor interpersonal skills and charisma will compensate for disinterest in one's work. Fight off the temptation to write off your future just because of a major setback. Keep the interest level up and avoid focusing on topics that wish for the end of the day, the end of the week, or the end of one's career, and do not keep the company of those that constantly remind us that life at work may not be very fulfilling. If you must think of retirement, do it in a positive way. Think how many years are left before one's own retirement and develop a list of ways one can make a unique contribution to the organization before this date. Then determine to work hard every day to achieve them.

9. Leave the past behind. Do not wonder about what would have or could have been if things had only worked out differently. Do not look back at the setback, look ahead with positive outlook. Worry will not help overcome the uncertainty of the future, willpower will. Keep the mind fixed on where one wants to go, not wavering backwards nor whining to oneself or others about an incident or situation from the past. There will be little or no sympathy from others anyway and there is likely nothing that can be done about it. "Worry is like a rocking chair. It only goes back and forth and gets us nowhere."

10. Resist all temptation to self-destruct. Stay away from the "fight or flight" responses when frustrated. One natural tendency is to react aggressively against the perceived source of one's discontent or to take ones anxiety out on others at work, home or elsewhere. Another natural tendency is to run away from the issue, a diversion tactic, and try to forget about it through the immediate gratification of alcohol, drugs, food, sex or other means. Any such response should be avoided at all costs, as giving in to any of these will only further complicate ones situation as well as be harmful to others and oneself.

Employees' Response

Managers need to realize the type of employees they have and consider what is needed to help them be the best they can be. Realizing the ten considerations for each type of employee provides a good start toward that understanding. All employees however, have a responsibility to rise to their highest levels of personal fulfillment and meet true needs, and working at one's best plays a vital role in this. Only the employee can ultimately control their attitudes and actions. The manager-employee relationship will depend on it, and indeed, employees can even be instrumental in changing managers to become better people and better managers.

Even the "Go-Getter" needs self encouragement and tips to stay at the top of their game from time to time. These individuals can be challenging to manage and are particular problems to the Power Managers and Marginal Managers, who view them as a threat. This is very unfortunate for these outstanding employees as their creativity and ability can become stifled. These same employees are a different kind of challenge to Employees' Manager. This manager must be careful not to show exceptional partiality and preference toward these outstanding employees as it may cause dysfunctional jealousy from the other staff. Rather this manager should simply continue to inspire them as well as all employees consistently toward improved performance.

The Employees' Manager knows to stay close to the action to see how everyone is working and contributing. This way the manager knows how the work is getting done and is able to assess the work climate. The Employees' Manager knows how to be patient and supportive of each employee as they strive to become better, and to look for their strengths and bring out their best. They are able to develop capabilities and generate qualities and strengths that employees did not know they even had. These managers elevate the performance and ability of each employee while making work fulfilling.

Chapter 7

Controls: Improving Performance and Accountability

Over the past several decades there have been many new laws, circulars, and orders promulgating rules and regulations to improve organizational performance and accountability in business and government. The ultimate objective is to clarify what organizations must do to be able to measure financial performance, productivity, quality of service, program and internal control performance, and the efficiency and effectiveness of service. Whether in the private or public sector, performance measurement is critical toward maintaining organizational controls and effective management decision making.

Performance Measurement

One of the first steps toward improving performance and accountability is to establish a performance measurement system that ensures and supports controls. Marlene Davies and Elaine Shellard[14] in their article entitled "The Value of Performance Measurement in the United

---

[14]M. Davies and E. Shellard. The Government Accountants Journal: The Value of Performance Measurement in the United Kingdom, Fall-1997.

Kingdom," point out that performance measurement is essential for control and accountability because it serves to:

1. improve service delivery;
2. demonstrate efficiency;
3. identify goals within departments;
4. help motivate personnel achieve their objectives;
5. aid management in assessing staff performance;
6. indicate to outsiders that money is not wasted in the public sector;
7. provide a standard by which to gauge the change in level of activity from one year to another;
8. provide a comparison with other organizations;
9. provide a base from which to assess activities when preparing tenders for work; and,
10. give objective quantifiable measures on which to judge performance and value-for-money.

This chapter critically examines the federal government's effort to achieve these objectives through the programs that have resulted from the 1983 Federal Managers' Financial Integrity Act (FMFIA), the 1994 Government Performance and Results Act (GPRA), and the 2002 OMB Program Assessment Rating Tool (PART). While this focus is on the Federal government's effort to deal with the reform of complex organizations, some of the same types of challenges and difficulties beset the private sector and the lessons learned below can apply to business as well as government managers as they attempt to gain better control, and improve performance and accountability.

The Battle against Fraud, Waste, Abuse and Mismanagement

The Federal Managers' Financial Integrity Act (FMFIA) and OMB Circulars on Internal Controls (A-123) seek to safeguard the federal government against control fraud, waste, abuse and mismanagement. The problem with the Act and circular is it did not establish internal controls standards and internal controls objectives for correcting problems after identifying them. These are significant shortcomings. For example, the problems generated by pork barrel politics (where projects are wasteful in their very nature), or with overstaffing, or lack of cost-effective contracts for services, or needless procurements of products or services represent the greatest waste of government resources. FMFIA and A-123 do not facilitate detection against those items that Federal employees see clearly as wasteful. Moreover, they do nothing to prevent the gross and continuous resource mismanagement of government.

It is also important to realize that government is a massive bureaucracy with self-perpetuating institutions. No private sector business could last long if it was as obtuse as most government organizations. That is, the government culture breeds unnecessary growth and waste which is perpetuated by its managers whose first priority it is to maintain or improve their own positions of power. Typical examples of unnecessary growth and waste throughout government are:

1. Managers tend to upgrade lower classified positions in order to promote the most competent and loyal employees into supervisory positions.

2. Managers and budget staffs are rewarded for their success in requesting and acquiring resources for the organization, regardless of demonstrated need.

3. Managers travel frequently for site visits and conferences which serve as social outings (renewing relationships), a free vacation, an uplift of ego and morale, and the benefits of pocket money gained from saving on food expenses and frequent flyer miles.

4. Managers want to make their office places as attractive and comfortable as possible, and seek the biggest office possible, and buy the best furniture, pictures, and office accessories. Managers typically only want them for themselves but will supply the entire office if necessary to justify it for oneself. When moving into new space or whenever surplus funds are available, they want the office space to be more open and roomy, and to give a plush appearance. To do this, they will redesign, renovate, and rearrange perfectly fine office space, repaint recently painted walls, carpet recently carpeted floors, and replace new drapes.

5. Managers want to be considered "progressive" so they will buy the most recent PC hardware, software, and peripheries and laptops, and media equipment possible, and update them as frequently as possible to "stay current."

6. Managers, organizations, and agencies will almost always find a way to spend whatever money given because they know if they do not spend it in the current year; they will not get the chance to spend it the next year.

7. Congress will give money to programs they believe are needed and never look to see if the programs did what they had hoped would be done.

8. Organizations fail to benchmark for higher expected performance than the status quo and when benchmarking is used, it is only to set lower performance targets and justify acquiring more unnecessary expenditures. Additionally, program outcomes are ignored; hard data is not created to confirm program impact; and programs expand merely on the belief that the program is working, or might work with more resources. Consistent Congressional support without accountability creates program conditions for continuous excessive waste and abuse.

9. Organizations grow annually without a review of productivity by either the organizations' evaluations or those by their Departmental oversight staffs. Essentially, the government has no effective program evaluation component for measuring cost-effectiveness.

10. Managers grow staff and resources by asking for "one-time" budget requests with the intent to convert to base budget increases, as soon as possible. New political

leaders appointed as organizational heads are neither versed in budgeting or performance, and fall privy to those senior managers who are gifted in the power of persuasion and marketing, rather than their managerial skills and program productivity.

Complex organizations have self-perpetuating mechanisms toward further future growth. That is, once established, programs tend to expand naturally from within as a means of self-preservation. This natural tendency has practical consequences...it raises costs and drives down productivity. For example, organizations try to retain its best employees by ensuring promotion potential but do so by creating new supervisory positions and small specialized staffs. Supervisors of small staff then gain status and promotion potential through the acquisition of additional staff, not performance. Their greatest effort is given to the imaginative justification of the need for additional staff.

With the increase of supervisors and staffs, the overall workforce naturally grows. The proliferation of smaller specialized units requires a level of management to manage managers. Slowly, the chain of command lengthens as the span of control expands. The more the top manager is removed from the action, that is, the more vertical steps up the hierarchical ladder to receive feedback, the more problems will exist in system operations and the more difficult it will be to implement reforms needed.

While human beings go through a natural deterioration

process with age, organizations have a built-in resistance to entropy. The chain of command from the line staff level to the top person in the organization typically gets longer as institution gets older and bigger. As the workforce grows, so does the horizontal and vertical communication chain within the organization. As a result, many interrelated problems develop that hinder decision making, productivity, communication, and creativity. The process to move ideas, decisions, actions, evaluations, and corrections then become difficult to develop, gain consensus, coordinate, and implement.

The longer the vertical/horizontal bands within the organization, the more likely most new ideas will die of neglect or malnutrition. Ideas that must be coordinated across or up too many layers loose meaning and integrity, being altered in substance with each step it goes beyond the originator. The approval process for memos can become an exercise where managers compete in their ability to edit, and to make the end product be designed simply to promote the status quo. By the time a memo gets to the top, the message potency has typically become so diluted and convoluted that the originator views it as irrelevant. Inevitably, the tendency is for creative employees to simply stop trying to improve conditions and processes. They either settle into a comfort zone of acquiescence in hope for future change in managers or management structure, or leave the organization to find a job with a smaller organization more in tune with customer needs.

Many organizations in the private sector have abandoned

the cumbersome chain of command because it stifles creativity. Organizations on the cutting edge of electronics such as Intel, for example, have their executives sitting in cubicles open to anyone to come and share their ideas at anytime. A person can come with an idea to the senior executive and be told to stop what they are doing and start developing the idea immediately.

Basic Management and Budget Principles of Government

There are certain basic management and budget principles that exist in government that feed the underlying subculture of institutional self-perpetuation. These include the fact that:

1. Very few critical reviews of government ever lead to reducing the budget. The Office of Inspector General (OIG) and Government Accountability Office (GAO) audits, OMB performance reviews, private sector reviews and responses to Congressional inquiry only serve to provide justification for short-lived criticism and long-lived additional spending.

2. Money comes easiest to those organizations who know those closest to the money. Direct lobbying or talking informally with appropriation staffers "off-the-record" is the most common way organizations acquire resources which Departmental and OMB budget oversight staff have denied.

3. Cabinet level officials familiar with how to run effective

business operations are the most likely to provide vision, reorganization, and control of government spending within their organizations without being forced to do so.

4. The greatest budget struggles in government should be between organizations seeking money and those Department budget staffs in charge of providing recommendations to Cabinet leadership. As long as there is no effort by Department staff to critically review organizations' cost-effectiveness because Congress will override decisions made, then there is little hope to constrain budgets.

5. Budget control at the Cabinet level is configured in any of a number of ways, with as many as seven levels of review and authorization, and typically as a result, the ability to make rational choices with full information on programs by top Departmental officials is almost non-existent.

6. The greater Congressional micromanagement and less autonomy afforded organizations, the less likely real organization reform can be administered. For example, Congressional authorization language for some organizations calls for notification and prior Congressional approval for actions such as reprogramming, reorganizations, and office relocations. This adds greatly to the ineffectiveness of government and enables a "do nothing" attitude to be instilled within the organizations and Departments of government.

7. The best way to control spending is by government

cutbacks across the board, but administered at the organizational level and at their discretion. A 5, 10, or 15 percent reduction if made at the discretion of the organization is an effective way to manage cutbacks. Additionally, a "no net growth" proposal allows increases proposed during budget formulation requests only if offset with equivalent proposed decreases.

8. There needs to be some common sense rules for the interpretation of performance indicators by budget staffs. Otherwise, there budget staffers use positive performance indicators as a rationale that the organization can do more with less and do not need resources; and negative indicators can be used to prove organizations do not deserve resources because they cannot be trusted to use the funds wisely.

9. It is an a fact of life that the best way for an organization to get resources is to royally screw up important missions or score poorly on highly visible OIG and GAO audits causing public embarrassment. When mission areas are considered "too important to fail," Congress will pour on the resources when and once the problems are made public. Certain organizations have elevated this to an art form as a way to grow their organizations.

10. The proof of performance in the achievement of goals as link to the level of resources used, namely the measure of cost-effectiveness, is rarely if ever examined in government. Pouring money for additional construction, equipment, staff, and technology does not necessary make organizations better. Moreover, when an measure of

performance threatens to risk a cut off of spending, the program accountability by this measure is terminated.

There are numerous corollary concepts that follow the same logic as to the inner workings of government and why the basic subculture tends toward self-perpetuation. For example, there will be a greater growth rate the closer one is to those that control the budget, applies to relations within an organization as well. Headquarters and regional offices which control resources have greatest access and understanding of the budget process and often take more than their fair share of the total pool of resources within the organization. This leads to a greater incremental growth rate than other parts of the bureaucracy, and this "piling on" effect means management requires more resources to do the same work. As staffs expand horizontally and vertically across the organizational chart, organizational rigidity in policies and procedures increase causing dysfunctional bureaucratic grid-lock up and down the chain of command. The greater the resources devoted to the highest levels, the worse the overall efficiency of the organization, as leaders become more mired in coordination difficulties.

What is bad for cost-effectiveness and productivity is not always bad for employees. Organizational dynamics are such that Headquarters and field units carry on an unstated exchange relationship that provides mutual benefits to each. As long as "the troops" in the field continue to get easy promotions and overtime pay, the HQ can get more positions and a higher portion of staff with large salaries. With this exchange, both are satisfied; field personal get extra benefits while Headquarters gets power and status.

Self-perpetuating mechanisms of organizations create a Catch 22 situation when it comes to reform whereby most reform efforts are doomed from the outset. Efforts to initiate reform to control growth often require more growth to implement the reform effort. Ironically, career managers and line staff see eye-to-eye on resisting reform efforts, as both have become wary of all new governmental initiatives, believing that reform only creates more meetings, paperwork, and unnecessary work for all. As field managers comply with the reporting requirements that make it appear as if real change is occurring, Headquarters middle managers provide the necessary cover, giving "lip service" to their superiors that things are moving forward. This way both the top executives and the production staff are fully insulated from any extra work or change, while the rest of the middle management makes it appear they have made real change when only pro-forma change has occurred if any at all.

Another factor leading to creeping growth is simply a function of political reality. Appointed political heads of organizations, despite their lofty ambitions, are by the nature of their newness, not typically informed enough to be optimally effective, not for almost two years. They can either make quick decisions that may not be the most informed or wait until they understand the situation, but at this point, their chance to motivate employees looking for sweeping change has past. Facing full scale organizational inertia, their sense of focus generally shifts and they begin thinking of their next job. Like steering a ship, sharp turns are difficult. By the time the top executive really knows what to do, they feel obliged to continue to rely upon the current managers who may neither be capable nor willing to carry plans forward.

The problem of not being prepared for the job lies not just with top management such as political appointees but often senior and middle managers who come into their positions not because of their leadership ability, but as a payoff for loyalty or some friendliness shown. Many new senior managers have shown no leadership ability, have met no prior management challenges, have rarely made any difference in any organization, and have little interest in their tasks or in the people they will be managing. Unfortunately, these are often the same people to whom the task usually falls to implement government reform. In short, the process of fighting fraud, waste, and abuse as well as conducting inspired planning and execution and instilling performance measurement and program evaluation, have a very steep uphill battle to work in a cost-effective manner in the government environment.

Implementing Measured Planning and Performance

Despite the many constraints of implementing reform in government, there have been many efforts undertaken and many lessons learned. The longest lasting of its kind, the Government Performance and Results Act

(GPRA) was designed to mandate planning and performance measurement, reporting, and monitoring. The GPRA calls for the development of long range strategic plans and short range performance plans for the tracking of performance results and program outcomes.

Under the GPRA, organizations are told what to do, not how to do it. Congress fearing that many organizations had become unaccountable, mismanaged, and may even have forgotten their mission, passed GPRA to focus on results, not on process. Congress has sometimes expressed little confidence in organizational leaders that do not know when their organization may be steering off course, or cannot prove whether they are operating effectively or cost-effectively. Unfortunately, organizational leaders often come before Congress requesting resources without a plan or knowledge of how successfully they are meeting their mission, and without data to prove what impact they have had on the problem they were created to solve or control. Organizations cannot begin to prove their worth without measures that track program results and outcomes.

The GPRA was passed with a five year pre-implementation phase to allow organizations plenty of time to get prepared to comply with the new features of the law. Organizations were further prodded toward the objectives of GPRA by OMB's Government Management Reform Circular and the National Performance Review (NPR), which promoted a similar emphasis on planning and tracking of results. Unfortunately, as GAO has reported on several occasions to Congress, Federal organizations are having a tough time seriously implementing the statute.

Part of the problem is that in order for GPRA to work, it must overcome the collective doubts of Federal managers' and their mental preoccupation with the failure of many previous reform efforts tried in the past. The prior effort to implement Management by Objectives (MBO) years earlier, for example, is a lot like the attempt by GPRA. As with any reform effort, there are many implementation issues that senior managers struggle with regarding GPRA. It is important therefore to understand the full meaning of the legislation and how it differs from past management reform efforts.

1. What is required by GPRA?

By authority of the original GPRA statute, Section 3 requires agency heads to submit a strategic plan to OMB and Congress, by September 30th, 1997; and Section 4, requires an annual performance plan and report beginning October 1, 1998 and Program Performance reports by March 31, 2000.

2. What is required in a Strategic Plan?

The law calls for a strategic plan that covers a period of "not less than five years" and "revised every three years." In preparing the strategic plan, the agency "shall consult with the Congress, and shall solicit and consider the views and suggestions of those entities potentially affected by or interested in such a plan."

As defined in the statute, the strategic plan consists of:

- a comprehensive agency mission statement covering the major functions and operations of the agency;
- general goals and objectives, including outcome related goals and objectives, for the major functions and operations of the agency;
- a description of how the goals and objectives are to be achieved, including a description of the operational processes, skill and technology, and the human, capital, information, and other resources required to meet those goals and objectives;
- included in the plan required by section 1115(a) of title 31 shall be related to the general goals and objectives in the strategic plan;
- an identification of those key factors external to the agency and beyond its control that could significantly affect the achievement of the general goals and objectives; and,
- a description of the program evaluations used in establishing or revising general goals and objectives, with a schedule for future program evaluations.

3. What is required in a Performance Plan?

The GPRA requires an annual agency performance plan to be submitted to OMB that covers all major program areas within the agency. The plan shall:

- establish performance goals to define the level of performance to be achieved by a program activity;

- express such goals in an objective, quantifiable, and measurable form or if not possible to quantify, in descriptive statements that define a minimally effective program and a successful program;
- briefly describe the operational processes, skills and technology, and the human, capital, information, or other resources required to meet the performance goals;
- establish performance indicators to be used in measuring or assessing the relevant outputs, service levels, and outcomes of each program activity;
- provide a basis for comparing actual program results with the established performance goals; and,
- describe the means to be used to verify and validate measured values.

4. What is required in a Program Performance Report?

The Program Performance Report consists of a completed report on organizational results for the past year, including those for performance indicators established in the agency Performance Plan, and the outcome of performance achieved for the previous year, or two years beginning in 2001, and three years starting in 2002. The law states that each report shall:

- review the success of achieving the performance goals of the fiscal year;
- evaluate the performance plan for the current fiscal year relative to the performance achieved toward the performance goals in the fiscal year covered by the report;

- explain and describe, where a performance goal has not been met (including when a program activity's performance is determined not to have met the criteria of a successful program activity.....why the goal was not met and the plans and schedules for achieving the established goal, and if the performance goal is impractical or infeasible, why that is the case and what action is recommended);
- describe the use and assess the effectiveness in achieving performance goals of any waiver; and,
- include the summary findings of those program evaluations completed during the fiscal year covered by the report.

5. How is GPRA different from the old Management-by-Objectives (MBO) program or the National Performance Review (NPR) reinvention activity?

The MBO initiative was implemented back in 1975-1976. Much like the PPBS (Policy, Planning, and Budgeting System) before it, and ZBB (Zero-Based Budgeting) after it, it had a short existence. MBO was very different from the NPR reinvention in both its spirit and substance. MBO focused on relatively static improvement processes, that is it attempted to improve what we are already doing, and took a micro management approach such as in the tracking of monthly personnel staffing to achieve a hiring objective. NPR and reinvention activities focused on improving processes or making structural changes including policy simplification and mission realignments for long term improvement.

GPRA is being implemented in a similar manner by many managers who remember what it was like to implement MBO. Unfortunately, these managers are comfortable with it for all the wrong reasons. They believe it is intended primarily as a status report on things reported before (such as workload data for the budget), and is therefore no more than a report on how well things are being done. Instead of a chance to rethink and reinvent, to overcome the inertia of major bureaucracies, and to remove barriers, the focus can quickly become just another budget exercise or organizational accomplishment report. This interpretation precludes the organization from undergoing or even exploring any potential areas for serious improvement.

6. What happened to MBO and were there any lessons learned that can help with GPRA?

MBO submissions became more detailed and swollen in size, and in the process the real issues became clouded. When the decision maker becomes lost in the forest of trees (the details can quickly become overwhelming to even the most enthusiastic reviewer), the process shuts down. Meetings are helpful to better understand the status of organizational progress and activities, but as a process, it tended not to lend itself to significant decision making, but only consumed enormous numbers of staff workyears in the preparation of meetings and development of reports. Thus, MBO was mostly a failure of the system to meet the appropriate need level of its organization and Department Heads.

The primary problem is the MBO material reflected the status of outputs and activities and not outcomes. MBO attempted to make incremental improvements, while the reinvention method, in comparison, attempts fundamental, long lasting impacts. Due to other organizational restraints and countervailing forces, the net result that often occurs with the incremental approach is that productivity and cost-effectiveness declines because the bureaucratic forces against improvement (such as organizational culture and climate) frustrate and overpower the forces for improvement.

Even when MBO becomes institutionalized throughout the organization by a one-time, strong, high level or top management involvement, the effort most frequently leads to unintended consequences that are dysfunctional to the organization. For example, the demand for performance goals and measures leads to the development of performance standards and reporting at the production levels; which promotes a greater reliance on control and reliability of performance within the organization; which creates a rigidity of behavior and quickening of organizational defense of status; which results in unresponsiveness to customers/clients/service recipients and more complaints, and results in poorer overall service and performance.

7. How can the agency comply with GPRA without introducing MBO-like mistakes?

GPRA requires all Federal agencies to develop management systems that include strategic plans, that link to outcomes and goals, and which should guide the budget process. These are measured, tracked, and reported annually, and evaluated and adjusted, throughout as needed. The authors of GPRA have obviously lived though past government reforms and wanted to ensure that all angles of sound management practice were covered. They wrote the language in simple terms, with definitions spelled out, and gave organizations five years to prepare for its implementation. What MBO left unstated, GPRA left little room for confusion. MBO was intended to be what GPRA is stated to be on paper. The problem is how to make the GPRA intentions a reality. While the law states what is needed through GPRA, it does not say how to do it.

What made the MBO process fail in the past is the same thing that could make the GPRA process fail: a process that misses the mark by concentrating on the wrong issues and concerns, overwhelming the organizational and Departmental Heads with unimportant detail. The focus should be on policy evaluation and mission cost-effectiveness, that is, determining what organizations should be achieving and at what cost. Organizations over many administrations sputter and fail in their reform attempts because there is little self assessment of: whether programs are having an impact on policy problems for which they were created; or, whether the most appropriate policy options have been chosen based on cost-effectiveness results. In essence, if GPRA is to become anything more than MBO, then it must strive to determine whether programs are achieving their intended results in the most cost-effective manner.

8. What problems are bogging down the GPRA effort?

Although GPRA is a law and therefore is innately more powerful than previous reforms tied to any single Administration, it nevertheless has begun to suffer the same outcome. For example:

- GPRA has become consider as largely a "paperwork exercise" controlled and orchestrated at the Department level (with input from organizational budget staffs) to satisfy OMB and Congress and their staffers who pay little attention to it. GPRA was intended to serve as an impetus and means for developing management systems for continuous improvement at the organizational level, with on-going refinement of performance monitoring and improvement of operations, yet organizational leaders rarely see the report or know much of anything about GPRA.

- GPRA's implementation strategy was myopic in vision due to its focus at the agency level, well removed from the action, and because of its failure to evaluate and know if the important things are getting done; its failure to focus on the most important measures, that of cost-effectiveness and to know if the most appropriate things are being accomplished well; and the failure to show the summary logic of programs where inputs, outputs, and outcomes are tracked to understand changes in program processes and performance.

9. Considering the need for management improvement in government, what approach to the implementation of GPRA should organizations take to avoid problems of the past?

The implementation of GPRA needs to be founded on the principles and spirit of the NPR, with its emphasis on reinvention and long term continuous improvement. This is important regardless of whether the organization is in a phase of high growth, cutbacks, or no growth. In all of these situations, there are unique problems that make organizations more susceptible to problems of productivity decline, loss of mission focus, and other unintended dysfunctional consequences. The key to successful government reform is to implement it within an organizational context capable of supporting it. Some of what is needed is a bottom up transformation of organizations with the following:

- The goals and rules of behavior, such as standards of performance and internal controls, should be established by the production level staff with input from service recipients to mitigate against potential problems caused by goals and rules imposed entirely above the working level, and to strengthen commitment to improved performance.

- Policy change, program enhancements, and budget

requests are stimulated by problems, questions, issues, and solutions raised in cooperation with the production level (with input from service recipients) and balanced against real, not imaginary environmental constraints uniquely experienced by Headquarters at the national level.

- Headquarters staffs must operate within a simplified vertical and horizontal structure so that communication, decision making, and policy/program performance improvements can be made rapidly to meet production/service recipient level demands. (Ideally, there should be no more than four levels from line-staff to the top commander in the field and directly to the Deputy Director from that commander. Then within Headquarters there should be no more than six to eight equally sized staffs at the horizontal level at Headquarters or the national level.)

- Organizational management structures and functions should be designed in uniform fashion within the Department and across government. The management staff structure comes under a single Head, reporting to the top manager in the organization responsible for policy, planning, budget, information resource management, and evaluation. This staff would be responsible for implementing all government reform efforts and provide direction and oversight on the implementation of points 1, 2, and 3 above. This staff also provides automated decision support systems as appropriate to operations staff, analytical staff, program management, and top management. Top management, for example, receives data on ultimate outcomes of key performance indicators, and results of major new initiatives and process reengineering efforts. This staff also promotes change initiatives as needed and monitors progress of change implemented; organizes personnel for the change effort; and prepares a "report card" on the state of health of the organization. The report card would provide management feedback on:

- Vertical and horizontal relations within the organization;
- Feedback from recipients of organizational services;
- Status of process improvement efforts; and
- Progress toward the ultimate goals and outcomes of the organization.

10. What does GAO say about how to implement GPRA since they often asked to evaluate organizations' interpretation and administration of government reform efforts?

In their report, Executive Guide: Effectively Implementing the Government Performance and Results Act (GAO/GGD-96-118, June 1996), GAO found that three practices were critical in determining which organizations were doing well with their GPRA implementation. These were the:

- inclusion of organizational stakeholders;
- evaluation of both internal and external environments; and,

- alignment of activities, core processes, and resources to support mission-related outcomes.

These primary reasons for the successful implementation of GPRA in organizations is due to the application of principles of the NPR and using reinvention in conjunction with the demands of GPRA. It seems the two must be used together if a successful process is to be discovered.

Monitoring FMFIA and GPRA: OMB's Program Assessment Rating Tool (PART)

The Program Assessment Rating Tool (PART) begun in 2002 was designed as OMB's means to keep organizations moving forward with planning and accountability. The objective was to have full federal government participation, adding 20% per year, heading toward 100% participation over five years. While this goal was attained, the impact of the program was suspect throughout its existence.

As difficult as it may be to implement improvement in government, there is certainly room for improvement in PART for not long after implementation it was dubbed the "Particularly Annoying Ridiculous Tool." While the PART "departed" or was rather abandoned by the Obama Administration, it is worth reviewing in detail to determine what lessons can be learned as the PART did attempt to fill an essential government oversight role and will eventually need to be replaced by some similar vehicle for improvement. The focus is on how it (or something like it) could be improved to overcome its design and implementation flaws.

PART Design Issues

The PART consisted of 25 questions divided into four segments: program purpose and design (5 questions), strategic planning (8 questions), program management (7 questions), and program results and accountability (5 questions). Each question called for a response (explanation) and some empirical proof (evidence) with supporting documentation such as statutes, policy statements, contract agreements and memoranda of understanding, as well as budget reports, and evaluation studies or audits, etc. Programs were rated on things such as how clear and sound is the purpose and design; how measurable are long-term and annual goals; how effective is management; and, what progress is made toward goals.

For scoring the PART, each question within the four segments is given a weighted score that together adds to 100 percent within the segment. Then each segment is given a weighted score that also sums toward an overall score of 100 percent. Program results/accountability is scored the highest (50%) and strategic planning (10%) the least, with program purpose/design (20%) and program management (20%) each scored evenly.

Federal organizations typically received exceptionally low scores in the PART. This was not necessarily because of organizational failures, nor was it the result of

OMB uncovering the stretching, evading, or denying of truth by organizations submitting the PART. Instead, flaws in the PART caused the low scores, and contributed more to false impressions than accurate perceptions about federal government performance.

The PART had built-in design flaws by the nature of the wording of questions, and due to the fact that the answer of "no" to any question caused a reduction in the overall score. Part of the problem with PART is the underlying assumptions of the questions and its treating all programs alike. Thus, the PART:

- penalized effective programs by assuming the existence of deficiencies (e.g., "has the program taken meaningful steps to correct its strategic planning deficiencies (2.8)?"...and..."has the program taken meaningful steps to address its management deficiencies (3.7)?"

- penalized effective programs with strong program monitoring by mandating that all programs must have "independent" and "regular" external program evaluations (e.g., "are independent evaluations of sufficient scope and quality conducted on a regular basis or as needed to support program improvements and evaluate effectiveness and relevance to the problem, interest, or need (2.6)?"...and..."do independent evaluations of sufficient scope and quality indicate that the program is effective and achieving results (4.5)?"

- penalized programs with unique missions (e.g., "does the performance of this program compare favorably to other programs, including government, private, etc., with similar purpose and goals (4.4)?"

- penalized programs with exclusive missions without linkage to or dependence upon "partners" (a term OMB neglects to define) (e.g., "do all partners commit to and work toward the annual and/or long-term goals of the program (2.5)?"... and ..."does the program, including program partners, achieve its annual performance goals (4.2)?"

In addition, the PART failed to seek answers to the most fundamental questions such as "what is the goal of the program?" and "is it appropriate?" Effective program design, planning, management, performance, and evaluation must start from concise and comprehensive statements of program goals. Without a clear understanding of the goals, programs can continue being dysfunctional, counterproductive, and resource wasteful even with high PART scores.

Instead of starting with program goals, the PART focuses on ensuring that there are "ambitious targets and time frames for its long-term measures (2.2)" and "baselines and ambitious targets for its annual measures (2.4)." For the target to be ambitious it should "promote continued improvement and achievable efficiencies." Here the PART misses its chance to clarify to what extent performance targets can be influenced by budget requests. It is easy to set "ambitious" performance targets if resource increases are factored in.

The PART did ask if "budget requests are tied to accomplishment...and performance targets are clearly linked to budget requests (2.7)." From this question (and assuming a relation to 2.2 and 2.4 above), one can assume that resource enhancements can be factored into performance targets provided there is continued improvement in efficiency and cost effectiveness. If this is the case, OMB's intentions for government reform capability are probably somewhat unrealistic.

The PART was also problematic because it only defined achievement as forward progress. There was no mention of performance measures as a deviation from an ideal state or acceptable standards of performance. When everything is working as it is supposed to, when there are no failures, it is important to measure performance deviations as exceptions to the ideal. Measures of performance for targets such as zero escapes, zero assaults, and zero security breaches, for example, are relevant for assessing the effectiveness of performance targets in law enforcement, protection, and homeland security areas. The questions in the PART, however, only focus on performance targets that measure forward progress without consideration to measures of exception within no-fault tolerance operations. In the PART, anything short of forward progress is considered "lacking ambition," even operations lacking any failures.

Also, in the PART, while ancillary information could be used to support answers (i.e., documented evidence), there was no clear way to credit "unquantifiable" accomplishments, such as narrative accounts of organizational results or program highlights from annual reports, into the scoring of the PART. There was also no accounting for one-time program changes that impact future cumulative cost savings or cost-avoidances. Instead of factoring-in one-time impacts, only continuous improvements in efficiency and cost-effectiveness could generate a high rating.

In general, there were a variety of problems in the PART design. In order to score a perfect 100% on the internally inconsistent and flawed PART, an organization had to have a schizoid personality, needing to manage and plan deficiently in order to then show proficiency; forcing innately independent missions to be performed interdependently; and tracking measures needlessly that could otherwise be assumed implicitly. Additionally, a problem with the PART design was that some parts do not add up and other parts were missing, and many parts were unclearly defined leaving much confusion in interpretation.

PART Implementation Issues

While design problems can always be fixed, there are a variety of implementation issues that may be more difficult to resolve; several are addressed below.

Program Selection

In conducting a program assessment using the PART, the first step is to identify the parameters of what is to be reviewed. OMB provides instruction that what must be reviewed are programs "important and meaningful for management and budget... (where the) aggregate level of activities are meaningful for performance measures." While this provides ample flexibility, it provides little or no guidance. Large complex organizations can interpret this to mean the PART can be applied to any number of programs; as few or as many as desired.

Under such instructions, most organizations are likely to find the fewest acceptable number of programs allowed by OMB to apply the PART review. In so doing, organizations create a carefully selected amalgamation of program activities to represent overall performance within the organization, generating a set of targets and measures that will produce the highest PART score. This can result in a mix of activities that fails to reflect all programs within the organization, and may not even represent a majority of programs. Thus, the PART failed to provide a true program assessment of the organization, not even a true index, and scores could not be compared to other organizations because of the lack of consistent application and logical sampling of programs for examination.

Outcome Measures

OMB rightfully stresses the need for organizations to measure outcomes of performance. While outcome measures (the ultimate results of performance) are of vital interest, in the PART instructions, OMB only offered one example in its guidance, which relates to a program that provides a "tornado warning system." The outcome measures used in the example are "the number of lives saved and property damage averted." The outcome of a tornado warning system can alert folks to go to their basements or those who live in a mobile home park to hitch up and ride away if possible, but the truth is that no matter where a tornado blows through, it is sure to scorch the earth behind....and it sure is difficult to assess "number of lives saved and property damage averted" as an outcome of a tornado warning....no matter how strong the spin.

More seriously, since OMB does not seek a goal statement for programs in the PART exercise, the linkage between plans, measures, and outcomes is not established. Program managers that fail to have goal statements may believe they have no control of program outcomes, and thus may fail to measure and track outcomes. Managers may believe their program has any impact to prevent, deter, eliminate, or vastly reduce the problems it was created to address. In some cases, the organizational energy is so misdirected or concentrated on self-maintenance activities that the program manager cannot articulate goals and program actions actually directly impede the successful attainment of outcomes.

Time Frames

In program planning, the level of attention given to implementation almost always determines success. Consider for example, the schedule that OMB provided for implementing PART in 2003 (for the 2005 budget). Organizations received a sixty page guidance document via internet on May 5th; OMB examiners were provided training on it on May 6th; "government-wide" training was provided to those intended to implement it (i.e., program, management, and budget analysts) on May 8th and May 9th; and organizations were asked to complete PART reports and submit these to OMB examiners by "mid-May" (May 15th or 16th). Thus within five working days of the training or 9 working days of receiving the guidance, the PART was due to OMB. Additionally, no formal memos or written instruction was provided to department or organization Heads.

This tight time-frame prohibits any honest self-assessment and naively disregards the need and benefit of involving top management. Consider the time it takes to implement anything new within a large organization. At a minimum, it requires briefings of top management and senior managers; training, input, and consensus buy-in of program managers; horizontal and vertical coordination of PART responses within the organization including top management approval, and final coordination and approval through Department budget and performance oversight staffs.

In addition, the assumption by OMB was that all other organizational activity could continue to be done without interruption as a new activity was introduced. The fact is, for many organizations, the timing of PART's mid-May due date had to compete with several important budget priorities, such as: the 2003 budget allocations (being administered to field units); the 2004 Congressional budget authorization testimony and follow-up questions and answers; and the 2005 budget guidance and submissions. Thus, the timing of PART required it to take a back seat to other "real" budget matters. The hurry-up fire-drill approach used in the PART implementation served only to alienate all involved.

Impacts

The ultimate objective of PART is to improve government...making it more cost-effective. The problem with the PART in this regard is that it only scratches the surface and never gets under the skin of the organization. PART only affects the environment of the organization, engaging Headquarters' staffs, Department management/budget staffs, and OMB budget examiners. This makes the PART very insular and ineffective as a reform tool. No matter how it may appear as being integrated into budget documents or used for budget decision making, it has little or no real impact in improving the organization. The PART starts as a tedious exercise in bureaucratic report writing, continues onward as a conflict-ridden negotiation process, and ends with OMB scoring that often appears arbitrary.

In some ways, it can be argued that the PART defeats the very purpose it sets out to accomplish. Ironically, it forces organizational pundits into compromising positions within their own organizations where they must defend the very programs they know need improvement. The PART wastes a good effort at much needed organizational change, and instead solidifies management retrenchment against self-correction.

The PART was perceived as an OMB "offensive" and the natural organizational reaction was to become more defensive and protective of the status quo. Instead of an honest management self-assessment, the PART became more of a chess match with OMB examiners. Instead of real improvement, organizational energies were diverted into devising whatever words needed to help the organization score high, look effective, and dismiss with the PART.

Interestingly, the PART has one other unanticipated consequence. It helped new alliances be formed between management and budget staff within organizations and with their Department oversight staff in order to produce the highest scores for the PART. This momentary suspension in the traditional checks and balances within and between organizations was accomplished simply to fend off OMB.

Moreover, although OMB officials deny the claim, OMB did use PART as a tool to cut resources and deny or approve budget increases. The Performance Institute (GovExec.com, May 6, 2003- Daily Brief) noted that based on PART ratings: "on average, the President's 2004 budget proposal rewarded programs deemed "effective" with a 6 percent funding increase, and held those "not showing results" to less than a 1 percent increase." In reality, some of the worse PART scores may have been the direct result of inadequate funding, not mismanagement; the problem was that PART could not help anyone tell the difference.

In general, the PART had problems with data validity and reliability, and more work was needed in both its design and implementation. In order to provide an accurate measure of organizational performance and help achieve the ultimate objective, more cost-effective government, lessons must be learned from the PART experience. Criticism of the PART is not condemnation of the whole effort, but PART scores, even increasing ones from year to year as was the general result, are not likely to reflect improvements in organizational structures, processes, and functions, as much as improved report writing and a loosening of OMB subjective standards. The fact is that in adjusting to the PART, organizations merely found ways to explain and provide evidence that there were no problems with program purpose and design, strategic planning, program management, and program results.

Rewriting or Amending the Legislation

True government reform does not occur if the effort is insincere within the organization, and it will not succeed unless it is a necessary requirement for all organizations with specific goals and processes defined. Many organizations have ignored the spirit of the FMFIA and GPRA laws, rendering the effect of the laws meaningless. Even Departmental staff often express openly that these laws are merely "an exercise" to meet Congressional demands. Moreover, OMB does little to support government reform that was passed in a previous

Administration or by the partisan opposition. Legislators also have been disappointed to find that these laws have not seemed to help produce better controls on spending. Pressures to reduce government spending and debt will bring on-going scrutiny of government operations. What is needed is a comprehensive streamlined government management law to improve and replace a dozen or more overlapping and ineffective laws and regulations.

FMFIA and GPRA do not define processes, but call for assessments and reviews, Strategic Plans, annual Performance Plans, and performance indicators and suggest there be input from employees and external stakeholders, and an evaluation mechanism to ensure that it is effective. Congress did not mandate rigid processes because every organization's mission, structure, and capability is unique, and thought it would be better to let each organization create their own planning process than to dictate one. While this initially came as a relief to organizations, soon into the process of implementation, the lack of a common structure became problematic.

Unless there is a statutorily mandated system for planning *and* accountability, there will be little success with either. The process must be clearly articulated with a common implementation structure to support it. Absent this, effective planning and accountability grows more unlikely not only with the change in Administrations but the further into any Administration, as political appointees become cozy with their senior management team and objectivity is lost. Since accountability threatens interpersonal relations, it is always easier to do nothing.

By failing to define the planning process in detail, planning units remained without authority and planning processes without consistent structure, and due to the lack of common application, it was soon realized that little cause for planning and accountability processes were needed and they were not formalized. Organizational attention shifts away from planning and accountability as soon as any program or budget priority becomes a more pressing issue; and then the planning effort falls to the lowest priority, eventually being eliminated, with the planning pundit left like a lone voice crying in the wilderness.

Planning units fight middle management resistance as long as they can afford to do so, but eventually discover survival is a better idea. They find the easiest path is to resist the planning process instead of implementing it. Instead of being planning advocates, planners become the front line report writers to accommodate Departmental pressures to plan and be accountable, or at least to appear so on paper. The problem stems from the lack of authority for planners and lack of definition to the planning process.

With little support at the organizational, Department, or OMB levels, Congress eventually sees the truth that the whole effort is only a paperwork exercise and they are left searching for an alternative. Instead of success, even organizations that have made ambitious attempts to implement FMFIA and GPRA are overwhelmed. Even the best efforts have stumbled over the same problems, encountered the same seemingly insurmountable roadblocks, fought the same battles against management resistance, and have eventually given up.

The problem of implementation such as the failure to define processes does not mean that planning and accountability is impossible. Other past management reform initiatives such as Policy, Planning, and Budgeting (PPB), Management by Objectives (MBO), Zero-Based Budgeting (ZBB), and OMB's Management Reform/Internal Controls (A-123), have not provided guidance specific enough to succeed either, and have also failed. The good thing about FMFIA and GPRA is that much has been learned about the processes and difficulties of implementing organizational change in the federal government, and at the same time much has developed in the way of change facilitation and technological advancement.

Improving Organizational Process and Outcomes

Characteristics of the dynamics in a healthy organization include the monitoring of compliance to program and internal control performance standards, setting and tracking ambitious performance plans from each organizational unit annually, and closely watching the bottom line: productivity and cost-effectiveness ratios (cost per unit of mission-related work). This organization is successful, innovative and flexible and realizes consistent gains in performance, meeting performance plans with current or reduced budget levels. This organization pays attention to employee satisfaction, interviews all employees that are transferring or retiring, and listens carefully to employee input on ideas for improvement. Their managers solve problems at the root cause and experience high levels of employee satisfaction, morale and retention.

This organization keeps their focus on mission, plans, and accountability and managers make wise policy, program development, technology, staffing, and resource allocation decisions. This organization reorganizes structures as needed, reduces unnecessary management levels, keeps open communication channels, advances technologies wisely (particularly networks and information systems), and makes staffing ratios competitive with the best organizations in the public or private sector. The organizational culture is geared for success. Managers seek and reward employee ideas, fill top jobs with strong leaders, and effectively reposition ineffective managers into positions where they can benefit the organization.

Some ways to improve organizational process and outcomes are to:

1. *Develop goals, objectives, and tasks*

The highest level of planning keeps the direction and focus of the organization on the proper targets, quality outputs, and desired outcomes. If the organization simply sets goals, objectives, and tasks, it will continue to improve performance. Project plans, such as PERT/GANT charts, blueprints, etc., will occur naturally as an outgrowth of tasking. "Goals" and "objectives" are placed into the Strategic Plan, with each goal having one or more specific objectives. The goals are related directly to outcomes and may take years to reach; objectives can be attained in the immediate future, usually one year or less. Sometimes, objectives become performance standards and are raised higher or replaced with a new objective after attainment. Tasks are more specific than objectives, are accomplished in shorter time frames, and ensure the organization is moving progressively forward in the right direction toward meeting objectives and goals.

At the beginning of each fiscal year, each unit manager should be asked for their top seven new improvement projects that will be achieved within the base budget in the current year. Each project would be tracked by the manager's supervisor. The supervisor considers all unit managers' efforts and selects the top seven priorities to report onward to top management.[15]

In this way, each organization, and the agency of all organizations are able to systematically select their top

---

[15]By the selective narrowing and prioritizing of the list of projects, the planning process does not collapse upon its own weight and allows each higher level manager to selectively prioritize their top projects so the top manager views only the projects of greatest importance.

seven most important projects. Although the public would become aware of the top seven plans, the actual new plans that are being tracked for real improvement would be seven times the number of organizational units in a department (7xUnits). This process ensures a system that involves real performance improvement, tracking, prioritizing, and selective reporting regardless of budget increases or decreases. At year-end, a single report of all improvements within base budget by functional area is produced for the record and citizen feedback, by OMB/Management, via the Internet.

2. *Monitor performance, accomplishments, and requirements*

Performance measures show progress toward meeting the tasks, objectives, and goals. For the full picture of organizational performance, performance indicators need to be complemented by workload and workforce data, accomplishments, productivity and cost-effectiveness measures (usually expressed in ratios of unit performance). This type of data provides a baseline for comparing the overall organizational condition.[16]
Staffing and budget allocations need to be reviewed

---

[16]Organizations should track a select few outcome measures to make it easy to track organizational progress. These measures should reflect effectiveness, efficiency, timeliness, and cost-effectiveness and be used to help operational, analytical, and management staff evaluate the success of their programs.

annually with the objective of stimulating improved performance and producing a fair distribution. Staffing and budget allocation recommendations should be made by a select team of organizational unit managers. Their decisions are based on a review of each unit's workload demands and staffing complement (using multiple regression or work measurement analysis), performance plans and standards compliance, and budget requests. The emphasis should be to redistribute staff to create the most equitable allocation of staff based on workload demands.

Resource standards are developed for each new position by type that includes a wide range of necessary budget expenses. The emphasis should be to redistribute increasingly leaner budgets and then by pooling funds from paring the budget down, innovative projects by proven managers would get funding. This pooling of resources promotes managers to be creative, to produce more within the base budget when no additional funds are available, and yet produce more effective performance plans with greater compliance to operational standards.

3. Set performance standards

Organizations need to establish essential program and internal control performance standards. These standards help the organization met its goals. All organizations must maintain at least a minimally acceptable level of performance in order to accomplish missions and survive. Performance standards are identified and tracked at the unit level and independently reviewed by Headquarters and audit staffs.

The Performance Plans of organizational units are the unit's basic business plans for the current year. They serve to ensure that each manager completes an annual review and certification of compliance to performance standards, where the standards can also be revised to ensure that basic missions are being accomplished in the most effective and efficient manner. Only those performance standards that are integral to the meeting of goals need to be identified in the report to top management.

The foundation of confirming effective, efficient, timely, and cost-effective operations is based on the development of minimum acceptable standards in all primary mission areas. Standards for acceptable performance should cover the core program areas. If an organization has eight programs, it is reasonable to expect each should have ten most critical internal control performance standards or approximately 80 altogether. The standards should cover all major program responsibilities, be measurable or able to be verified, and not overlap. Once standards are set, they will strive to be attained. Once attained, they are usually maintained.

4. *Develop performance and budget plans*

Each senior executive manager of a program or staff should submit a performance plan to the organizational Head, containing the seven new accomplishments planned for the current fiscal year within the current base level of resources. The plan should be in rank order of importance as perceived by the manager and identify each task under the objective to which it applies. Performance Plans are designed to get the most out of organizations within their current level of resources. Organizational units should get a chance to request resource enhancements (one to three ideas for new positions and funding) only after given the opportunity to describe what new initiatives they are going to undertake within their current resources.[17]

Only limited budget requests should be made by each organizational unit annually, with performance awards being reserved for managers and organizational units that do more with less. Managers that receive an increase of staff or resources need to identify those tasks that will be accomplished as a direct result of the increase. After performance indicators have been set, seven point plans have been developed, and ten program/internal control standards reviewed for compliance and planned corrective action, then the budget request and review process begins.

---

[17] When plans are always dependent upon additional funding, managers feel justified in not meeting existing challenges and rather than being creative, cutting costs, becoming more efficient, etc., they defend the status quo and refuse to take needed actions to improve within their current base budgets.

As each organizational unit submits their top three plans for budget enhancement, the plans should not overlap plans previously proposed in the performance plan. These budget plans are reviewed in conjunction with the performance plans. Emphasis is on rewarding managers with a successful performance plan implementation record and effective prior use of new funding.

5. *Ensure accountability*

Accountability begins with a report schedule and consequences tied to results.

- Organizational Heads should be required to report to the Department Head every four months to address progress on the Performance Plan;

- Organizational Heads need to meet with Headquarters' program managers one week before each of these meetings;

- Organizational unit managers need to report to the Director every six months on the details of task accomplishment; and,

- Program/unit managers need to update progress toward task accomplishment into a central data base as the task is completed on an on-going basis.

A system of real rewards and sanctions need to be created and tied to performance.

The top three executives and all senior managers must have quality executive information systems and be expected to track plans quarterly. If performance is tracked, it will be improved. If managers get appropriate, accurate, and timely data, they can manage operations effectively. If all budget, policy, program, personnel, and reward decisions are made on the basis of information from a quality data base, employees improve performance. Tracking performance improves performance only when top management uses the information persistently and continuously refines data quality, decision making, and communication feedback systems.

6. *Monitor and report on implementation*

The organization's Management and Planning staff provides planning guidance and support to the organizational Head and unit managers and serves as liaison with the agency planners. This staff monitors progress, analyzes weakness and strengths in participation, and provides summary reports and positive feedback to the top manager on accomplishments, and also designs the linkage or integration of planning and performance management with budget formulation, execution, and resource allocation. This Unit also tracks organizational unit reports (every six months) and attends status report meetings (every four months) with the Director and each program manager, and identifies plans that require cross-organizational coordination, chooses primary leader roles, differentiate tasks for each organizational unit, and tracks the implementation of these plans separately from the other plans.

Executive reports and meetings should be standardized and kept to a minimal. Once the above system has been put into place, reports to top management can usually be reduced several-fold from preexisting crisis reports. Executive meetings can be minimized and be very meaningful, with expectations clear. Data collection systems can be revised without the uncertainty of what information is needed, and thereby data input and collection is simplified significantly. Accuracy and value of the information system will also improve.

Managers should not be overburdened with oral or written reports. While the following report requirements could be expressed in person or at group meetings with the top executive, an e-mail to the same individual or designee would be sufficient. Each report need not be longer than one page in size. The timing and types of management reports could include the following:

Immediate Response:
- Provide immediate notification of major incidents, problems, or issues of significant or potentially significant impact.

Weekly Report:
- Provide status of major incidents, problems, and issues and corresponding response plans, and any completed projects/improvements identified in the performance plan.

Monthly Report:
- Provide progress made on three or fewer major projects provided funding enhancements in current year.
- Provide a summary of organizational units where there are greatest problems and what is being done about it.

Quarterly Report:
- Using simple cost-effectiveness indicators for major organizational units and programs.
- Compare current status of performance against prior quarter, past year, and current plan.
- Provide brief progress report on status of seven-point performance plans.

Semi-Annual Report:
- Compare progress on program and internal control performance standards against prior half year, past year, and current year plan.

Annual Report:
Summarize end-of-year progress toward meeting plans, including:
- Cost-effectiveness performance indicators;
- Programs performance standards and internal control performance standards;
- Seven point performance plans; and,
- Extent of goal accomplishment for any newly funded projects.

7. Reach inside-out for ideas leading to improvement

Employees' input is vital to the success of the organization because employees are the first to know what is wrong with the organization and often how to best improve it. All employees should participate in a structured planning process at the program or unit level. The process should occur annually for the development of the Performance Plans. Each manager should ask employees to assess the success of the program or unit and make recommendations. The input gets factored into the Performance Plan, and corrective actions are taken and tracked throughout the year. A managers' success is largely dependent upon employees' willingness to be actively engaged in the planning effort and committed to the implementation effort.

Additionally, every three years the organization should conduct a long term trend analysis, looking at demographics and mission related measures, and seeks to identify potentially needed changes in policy, program, and resources. This analysis should guide budget formulation, include input from Congressional oversight staff, OMB examiners, and stakeholders, and focus on areas of consensus and conflict of outlook. Policy guidance statements are then prepared that guide the Strategic Plan, the Performance Plans, and budget formulation.

Every two years, each organizational unit should also request formal feedback from employees, customers, suppliers, clients or partners. This input is used to develop/revise performance standards, plans, goals, and process improvements throughout the year. The employee feedback should consist of ideas to improve quality and cost-effectiveness of the organizational units as well as provide feedback on improving programs, and their assessment of regional and Headquarters' responsiveness and support.

At the same time, evaluation feedback on managers' performance is needed for all program units. A "report card" on program managers is used to assess responsiveness, service, innovativeness and accomplishment of plans; monitoring and fulfilling performance standards; and customer, supplier and employee feedback, including a survey of employee climate and satisfaction. The organization's Management and Planning Staff can survey all field unit managers for their impressions of Headquarters performance and random clients/customers for an assessment of field unit managers.

8. *Develop policy guidance and vision upfront*

The Department Head should provide a brief statement of priorities each year to initiate the current year performance planning process. To serve as input to this guidance, each organization's Management and Planning Staff provides input/feedback on their assessments of future requirements and current issues within/outside of their organization. Top management is interviewed for their assessment of program priorities. Once the "white paper" is released, the Departmental priorities are factored into all layers of organizational planning, performance, and budget operations and provides essential input for prioritizing and organizing work performance.

9. Keep the plan alive

There are certain qualities that make plans work well or not effective at all. Plans that are overweight are also usually untimely and inflexible. That is, plans that take a long time to develop and are difficult to maintain have barely any chance of succeeding. Plans need to be easily organized and reorganized and should include: independent program areas; areas that cross-cut a few programs; and areas that apply to all programs. Plans need to be flexible, living documents able to be adjusted quickly to add new priorities, eliminate plans that are overtaken by events, and elevate or reduce emphasis on other plans.

Planning takes hold when: a) the manager in charge of overall planning is central to the senior management team and close to the Organizational Head; b) responsibilities and tasks are quickly and appropriately assigned to the proper managers; and c) managers are willing to readjust their activities as the Organizational Head's plans change. Plans important to the organizational Head need to be adjusted easily and monitored closely to improve organizational performance.

Planning and accountability are interdependent; without

one the other cannot be effective. Accountability is not possible without plans, and plans are not implemented effectively without accountability and consequences. Plans work well when there is: a) the ability to send updates to plans from the organizational Head quickly via e-mail; b) the ability to track plans centrally from a database whereby all managers can access and update progress on plans continuously or at least monthly; and c) the Organizational Head issues real rewards and punishments based on performance.

10. Develop performance management programs

Each organization should be periodically evaluated by Departmental management oversight to determine if process and outcomes are acceptable. The review should consider three levels of operation:

- The program performance plan level: How well did the organization meet its planned objectives and planned tasks, and how well was the effort to develop and evaluate these activities?

- The program monitoring level: How advanced is the organization in establishing program, process, and internal control performance standards, and how well were these tracked and used in making organizational decisions?

- The productivity, cost-effectiveness, and outcome level: How advanced is the organization in establishing productivity, cost-effectiveness, and outcome indicators and how well were these tracked and used in making organizational decisions?

Each cabinet and OMB/Management needs to establish a comprehensive performance management program for the Federal government. The program should emphasize the points above, as well as those principles expressed in the ten organizational priorities (TOP) model. OMB should also serve a critical role for disseminating best business practices to government organizations that can most benefit from them.

Every cabinet agency should be able to monitor the status of outcomes concerning a number of key indicators of success (maybe as few as a dozen) in order to measure the impact or success of resource enhancements or declines, or new legislation, policy, and program changes. The assessment of performance outcomes on missions provides feedback to OMB and Congress and facilitates informed change as needed. , An assessment of basic outcomes might give the Department of Justice, for example, answers to the following questions:

- what is the cost-effectiveness of our Federal law enforcement organizations, and the impact of resource increases to prosecution, detention, prison populations, and crime?

- what is the impact of bail vs. detention on community protection, court attendance, and the cost of fugitive apprehension?

- what is the impact of crime/drug legislation on general deterrence, and prosecution policy on immigration offenders on the expansion and reduction of the Federal detention and prison population?

- what is the impact of correctional policy on community corrections, prison construction, and recidivism?

- what is the level of unresolved Federal crime and amount of unexecuted Federal fugitive warrants and what is its impact on general deterrence?

- what is the impact of Justice Policy and programs on the prevention of crime and community social control, and in providing useful feedback to the other Federal Justice organizations?

- how does Speedy Trial Act compliance, prisoner processing practices, and the utilization of community alternatives affect Federal detention and costs?

Once these questions can be answered, outcomes could then be monitored over time as initiatives are implemented, and the impact of Departmental actions could be truly assessed.

The challenge confronting Cabinet staffs is to seek and

find ways to answer basic questions of mission and to better direct and organize policies, structures, functions, and energies in the most cost effective manner.

To ensure controls, government must improve performance and accountability. To assess progress in these areas, basic policy, program evaluation, planning, and monitoring are needed. The primary issue should not be financial management and accounting as is currently the case today. The issue is how to establish performance plans and measures with the primary objective to improve cost-effectiveness and implement cost-saving and cost-avoidance management improvements. Fragmented budget driven planning, untrained and unaccountable managers, and general bureaucratic resistance continue to make major improvements difficult. At this point, OMB and Congress needs to step in and undo the mess it created, and take on the challenge of reforming government seriously.

Chapter 8

Change: Reorganizing with Purpose

There are many types of reorganizations in business and government and just as many motivating forces. Reorganizations, in the ideal, are designed to improve organizational productivity and cost effectiveness as well as employee morale and working conditions. Managers, however, being human beings and possessing ultimate power within a limited setting, are often motivated by other factors. In fact, there are probably more reorganizations that are designed to accommodate parochial desires of the senior manager, than there are to improve organizations.

The primary motivating force for reorganizations can be something as simple as the desire of the top executive to push away threatening or socially repugnant people and bring loyal and physically attractive people closer to them. While this may be the real purpose of the reorganization, the senior manager will make every attempt to conceal it by incorporating a variety of other meaningless changes within the same reorganization. Whatever latent goals drive reorganizations, the true reasons eventually become apparent, and impacted employees then make informed adjustments.

Since reorganizations remain one of the most popular

exercises of authority by top management, this chapter examines how to assess if reorganization is needed and how to conduct a serious one if desired.

Reorganization Decision Process

Major reorganizations are designed to overcome the consequence of bureaucratic evolution that has produced unnecessary layers of management, unnecessary personnel linkages within layers of management and operations, inefficient communication, weak and delayed decision making, and diminished cost-effectiveness and performance outcomes.

The top executive almost always wants to "make an impact" and leave their imprint on the organization. Reorganizing people, programs, authority and reporting structures and organizational units is one of the most frequently used methods to do this. Reorganizations are an opportunity to rearrange and reinvent structure and work processes to improve organizational cost-effectiveness, service, and morale, and as such, can address a wide range of organizational issues along the way.

Determining whether to reorganize should be based on a number of considerations. Consider the TOP Model to know whether or not it is time for a major reorganization:

1. ***Leading with Leadership***
   - Are goals set entirely by top managers without

middle-management and employee input?
- Is top management provided sufficient feedback on front-line production or operations at the local or direct service level?
- Is there poor staffing, resource formulation, allocation, and/or execution?
- Is there acute dissatisfaction with the methods used for determining distribution of resources?
- Have spending decisions in the areas of greatest impact been unwise?
- Have unnecessary layers of management been created to support tangential missions in order to provide promotions to "rising stars" that need staff and responsibilities to become supervisors?
- Are there patterns of decision-making that seek to fix problems for the present only, neither taking into account the true immediate or long range needs of the organization?
- Do employee discipline problems get fixed by transferring trouble employees to other locations?

2. *Unity of Purpose and Plan*
   - Is there lack of clarity of mission, purpose or plan?
   - Is there a lack of congruence of perception regarding policy and goals at different hierarchal levels within the organization, as well with suppliers and customers or clients?

3. *Unity of Command*
   - Are there conflicts between managers or managers and employees that are destructive?

- Is the distribution of authority uneven among managers and if so, is it problematic?
- Do Headquarters' authorities control major decisions of personnel recruitment, evaluation, retention, and promotion, while Regional or field unit authorities is responsible for supervision of the same individuals' performance?
- Is information received by top management obstructed, filtered, and transformed in its meaning as it travels from its source so that top managers fail to receive essential information, and is there any message distortion going in the opposite direction from top to bottom?

4. *Unity of Effort/Culture*
- Is there inequitable work distribution and responsibilities?
- Is there insufficient control within the organization to ensure high standards of performance compliance?
- Do employees have a positive morale?
- Do employees genuinely support of organizational purpose does it reflect in productivity?
- Is there potential for nation-wide backlash of bad publicity for failure from a single local unit?
- Is employees' autonomy, growth potential, and pay structure comparable to outside competitors?
- Have former political appointees or transfers remained in management positions as a result of privilege rather than merit?
- Does management micro-manage operations?

- Are the local units closest to the suppliers and customers satisfied with their work relations and treatment?

5. Minimizing Organizational Structure
- Is the organization organized most efficiently?
- Is the organizational chart overly complicated with excessive links in the chain of command and broad spans of control?

6. Simplifying Workflow Process
- Are program responsibilities aligned in a logical manner?
- Do policies and procedures regarding operations seem excessive or insufficient, overdeveloped or underdeveloped?
- Do managers have authority to make changes in business practices to improve productivity?

7. Achieving Accountability
- Is there accountability for the achievement of pre-established goals, as well as work measure and performance targets?
- Is information on performance accessible and is it used by top managers to assess progress toward goals and conduct personnel evaluations?
- Are there adequate measures of performance in place to assess performance for all employee and manager levels?

8. Gaining Technical Proficiency
- Are there adequate internal controls and program

performance standards?
- Is the organization well equipped technically to handle the duties of the job?
- Are there enough specialists and sufficient training available for employees to accomplish the missions?

9. *Ensuring Quality Input and Output*
- How well is the organization performing?
- Do managers take responsibility for the cost-effectiveness of their operations?
- Are all organizational units performing at acceptable levels of quality and productivity?
- How satisfied are suppliers, customers, organizational oversight authorities?
- How able do managers' sense and response to new external demands and mandates?

10. *Assuring Effective Communication*
- How effective is the communication within the organization, vertically and horizontally?
- How effective is the communication with suppliers and customers?
- How effective is the use of e-mail, Intranet, and Internet communications for feedback and improvement?
- How organized and effective is the structure of manager/employee meetings for the sharing of information?

After a thorough preliminary problem assessment using the TOP model questions, the top executive will be in a good position to know if a major reorganization is needed.

Some Hidden Reasons for Reorganizations

It is not being cynical but sadly true that quite a high percentage of reorganizations are not intended to address the real problems within organizations, but result from the personal agenda of the top executive or of one or more conspiring senior managers with the top executive. Of course, all reorganizations will be announced as an attempt to improve the organization, no matter how nefarious the intent. The honest underlying reason is rarely openly revealed and sometimes not understood as such until much later.

The following titles of reorganizations denote the many prevailing themes if they were honestly revealed:

1. **Revenge Reorg:** This is done to replace managers that have been perceived as disloyal, not team players. The targeted managers and their employees' performance may not be a problem; the issue is that they have annoyed top managers by something they said or did, maybe disparaging, questioning, or doubting Top Management on their ability or integrity.

2. **Repayment Reorg:** This occurs when one manager is promoted to a position of authority over his/her previous boss and reorganization is "payback" for this offense. The targeted manager is typically put into a position without authority and little responsibility, and given the

office's menial work (known as the "penalty box" rotation) or no work at all (known as a "sabbatical").

3. **Retro Reorg:** Top management has finally departed sometimes after only a few years at the helm but often under some pressure and pretense, or actual problem. The Acting Official and Senior Managers conspire to change everything back to the way it was before the top manager arrived and before anyone new arrives, "when things worked better."

4. **Reshuffle Reorg:** When a new executive wants to reduce the power and influence of the senior managers, he/she simply switches them from the management of one familiar area to that of an unfamiliar area, with completely different employees of untested loyalties. In essence, this realignment or regrouping "levels the playing field," as the managers will need to start over to prove and reestablish their authority and support. Not only does their old power base evaporate, but the old cliques that served to support the manager's ego disappear as well.

5. **Repatriate Reorg:** A notable senior manager or former leader returns to a position prior held to fulfill the job that nobody seems equally capable of doing, causing a domino or ripple effect throughout the organization, with managers being bumped over or pushed down.

6. **Rendezvous Reorg:** The prime motivator of this reorganization is to promote into management a rising star (usually a former special assistant or personal

advisor and most often member of the opposite sex) into a favorable managerial position so they can advance the admired one's career and relish the continuous close contact or indebtedness it will afford.

7. **Rehash Reorg:** This is the resurrection of the long discussed, planned, and yet never implemented reorganization that everyone forgot about or thought had gone away. It is simply dusted off and implemented with perhaps only slight changes but can serve the legacy needs of a new top executive in quick order.

8. **Restitution Reorg:** This is the Man of La Manchu's solution for a reorganization, where past personal wrongs will be righted, where managers that should have been promoted finally are, and those that should never have been, are removed.

9. **Remedial Reorg**: This occurs when a new Top Manager looks at the status of performance by the organizational management team and decides the only way to get things right and to assure honest communication at the top is to replace them with one's own people from the outside.

10. **Reinvention Reorg:** This occurs after the use the TOP questionnaire or other assessment determines that major work, not minor work, is needed in an organization.

    This is the only reorganization that takes into account organization purpose and performance, cost/effectiveness, resource expenditures and outcomes, management productivity, work flow processes, organizational structures, and employee morale, salary and benefits. It not only results in the shifting of personnel and managers into new positions, but it consolidates structures and functional alignments, simplifies work flow and compresses work activities, clarifies and measures organizational purpose and outcomes, and increases productivity and employee involvement. This reorganization is responsive to major changes in the operational environment, legislation, budget availability, and executive mandates. In the private sector, it may be in response to a corporate buyout but it too has a rational underlying purpose and plan.

The Rational Reorganization

Any reorganization designed to produce fundamental change for improvement begins with the positioning of the best people in the top positions of the organization, proceeds by minimizing the complexity in structures, functions and work processes, seeks to improve management-staff relations and employee morale, and strives to greatly enhance performance and cost-effectiveness. The process of conducting a rational reorganization should consider the following:

1. Get Input. If the reorganization is to be successful, it must not only be a top management initiative, it must be the top manager's initiative. The top executive should first solicit input from employees of all levels to identify problem areas and recommendations for improvement, as well as issues and resolutions. Suppliers and customers should also be provided the same opportunity to give feedback. A trusted outside consultant might be hired to orchestrate the entire reorganization with the assistance of support team from within the organization that can be the top executive's primary point of contact. Employee suggestions and ideas can come directly to the independent source or to the top executive via formal and informal interviews, surveys, open forums, memos, e-mails, or telephone calls.

2. Announce Purpose. The top executive needs to have some guiding principles not be abstract ideas, about what end-results are desirable. These need to be stated so everyone can understand the objectives of the change. The following are some themes that the top executive has to offer as reasons for reorganizing:

- Improve performance in effectiveness, efficiency, timeliness, and cost- effectiveness;
- Enhance customer service and satisfaction;
- Increase employee empowerment, decision making authority and morale, particularly as it relates to the service delivery level;
- Improve employee accountability for performance;
- Cut red tape by reducing the number of agency policies, rules, and regulations;
- Reengineer operational and business practices;
- Reduce/realign headquarters or regional staff and resources, and refocus efforts from the role of controlling to that of planning, guiding, facilitating and supporting;

- Move toward smaller teams covering broader stretches of mission areas with a mix of specialists and generalist roles coming together to get the work done;
- Improve the information systems so that timely and integrated financial and program performance reports are produced easily on a regular basis; and,
- Better respond to the wishes or mandates of higher authorities outside the organization including the Department Head, OMB, the President, and Congress.

3. *Maintain Pace.* The independent consultant or reorganization project leader (and internal support team) keeps the reorganization review process moving ahead steadily and on-time, exploring opportunities for business process improvement, communicating progress and special challenges and impediments, and providing feedback to the organization through frequent e-mail announcements on how things are proceeding and to acknowledge and address anxieties that may exist.

4. *Focus on Customer.* A special effort can be made to learn from the customer what might be needed to better produce quality goods and services, perhaps by streamlining business processes and consolidating of similar functions to improve efficiency.

5. *Review Management.* Review managers' programs and reporting relationships (organizational charts, mission, function, and staff size); conduct staff analysis (by grade/salary, position description and personnel classification); examine performance plans, measures, and accomplishments (long term plan as well as intermediate and current year plans); review business practice and policy (flow diagrams of processes "as is" and "should be") and, review program and internal control performance standards.

Conduct one or two in-depth interviews with program managers to obtain impressions of what each manager perceives are the problems (within their area and other areas of concern) and their recommendations for improvements. Corroborate problem and issue areas with appropriate oversight review staffs, such as the Inspector General and other audit, planning, or analysis groups.

6. *Consider Repositioning.* Review responses from employee surveys, interviews, and feedback by program, and determine which types of managers are Employees' Managers, Power Managers, and Marginal Managers. This will differentiate which managers have the respect of their staff, have a clear sense of purpose, are assertive in decision making and action taking who appreciate their employees, and strive for the best performance possible.

7. *Measure Pre/Post.* Measure attitudes, relations, and program performance before and after the implementation of the reorganization. A survey should be administered to a broad sample of employees as early as possible before the reorganization announcement and before leaks about a potential reorganization become widespread (see example of survey at end of chapter).

The same survey should be administered a year or two after the reorganization has been completed. Organizational and unit performance should also be compared. The post assessment should determine its:

- completeness (did everything get done that was intended to get done?)
- accomplishment (did the problems get solved—and what was newly achieved?)
- cost-effectiveness (did cost per unit produced/services provided improve?)
- impact on manager/employee relations (did the social climate and employee morale improve?)

8. Develop Organizational Alternatives. The project leader prepares alternatives that set aside the concept of existing organizational configurations, including the vestiges attached to individuals and personalities presently in management positions, and present business practices that have "always been done that way." The alternatives include new structure and functional alignments with the advantages and disadvantages of the various proposals to impact organizational performance, employee morale, management oversight, and business practices. Recommendations are made in private to the Top Executive.

9. Reposition Appropriately. The top executive receives recommendations on the senior leadership positions in the newly selected or recommended configuration. The top executive makes a final decision on managers and staff allocations.

10. Implement the Reorganization. A team is established to direct and monitor the implementation process following a plan. This Plan shows how the organization would move from its current state to the future state. New and detailed organizational charts show the relocation of affected managers and employees, and a position control system is used to track movements. Special responsibilities and direction is given to Space Management, Personnel, Finance and Performance Management teams in implementing the change, ensuring locations, duties, personnel records and pay records are adjusted as needed, and that performance accounting during the transition is maintained.

Survey Assessment of Staff Perceptions

Responses:
- *a.   strongly agree*
- *b.   agree somewhat*
- *c.   not sure*
- *d.   disagree somewhat*
- *e.   strongly disagree*

<u>Satisfaction</u>

- Overall, I am highly satisfied working within this program area?
- The work I do on this project is interesting and

enjoyable.
- I believe our clients or customers are most satisfied with our group's efforts and work.
- While working on this program or project, management has treated me fairly.
- Is there anything else you would like to say that was not covered in the job satisfaction part of this survey?

Teamwork

- The working environment within this program area encourages worker cooperation to achieve staff goals.
- I'm proud to be a part of this program area.
- Working relations with those we service are excellent.
- All in all, comradely and team spirit within the staff is excellent.
- Is there anything else you would like to say that was not covered in the Teamwork part of this survey?

Efficiency / Effectiveness

- I think this program has been very effective at doing what those we service have asked us do.
- In your view, our efforts in this program are perceived as being very effective.
- I think our work in this program is very efficient and timely.
- I think our work in this program is very cost-effective.
- This program does quality work.
- With each successive month, the quality of work continues to improve.

- Is there anything else you would like to say that was not covered in the efficiency/effectiveness part of this survey?

Communication and Management Awareness

- Before decisions are made, the staff's opinion is requested and seriously considered.
- The employees are encouraged to apply innovative thinking and problem-solving in their duties.
- The employees feel they have meaningful impact on the practices, procedures, and the manner in which tasks are accomplished.
- The staff has clear objectives and guidance on what needs to be done.
- The staff does not feel alienated from or ostracized by their fellow employees who are not a part of this program.
- Management shares information about each other's policies, roles, concerns, and accomplishments so everyone knows what's going on.
- I believe that Top Management in my organizational structure is aware of my performance.
- Is there anything else you would like to say that was not covered in the communication and management awareness part of this survey?

Training

- I have adequate training to perform my job.
- I believe that training is available if I need it.

- What additional training, materials, or resources (e.g. data bases) do you need to do your job?
- Specifically, what improvements would you like to see in this program?
- Is there anything else you would like to say that was not covered in the training part of this survey?

Chapter 9

Structure: Optimizing by Standardizing

Most senior and many middle managers do not favor any organizational improvement efforts that may impact their areas of responsibility. Their influence, position, and existing relationships with superiors, peers, and subordinates are all based on maintaining the status quo. Any review or objective critique or effort toward improvement is viewed as a potential threat. With their status and success dependent upon the self-maintenance, any change to the existing conditions, relations, structures, or communication patterns is feared. The challenge of any major organization is to overcome the natural emphasis to operate as a closed system and to overcome stagnation and resistance to change by changing operations into open systems for the purpose of continuous improvement.

Continuous improvement is not the same as continuous growth; in fact in some organizations and throughout government, it should be the opposite. The nature of continuous improvement is doing more with current resources or doing just as good with lesser resources. In closed systems, change does not come voluntarily. The role of developing mechanisms to truly reform government, for example, will need to come from a loud and demanding General Public, the taxpayer, and be imposed by OMB and Congress. Unfortunately, every effort so far to reform government has inadvertently led to more growth, waste, and inefficiency. With little confidence that government is capable of reform and with the growing debt and the budget deficits, basic structures need to change in order to change the nature of government's continued growth, inadequate accountability, and insufficient performance.

That is, the size of the government needs to be permanently reduced by eliminating unnecessary layers of the management structure and standardizing management functions and practices. Government can work better, fitting closer to its constitutional purpose, if it were much smaller and better organized with a minimum structure that would ensure it stays limited but effective and efficient.

Standardize Basic Structure

In large organizations, cut in half the span of control and chain of command at Headquarters and at all major field units, and eliminate regional offices and the sub-offices of field units entirely. The new reporting relationships would include the following:

- All large organizations (with 4,000 employees or more) should have no more than six senior managers and major program areas (three administrative and three operational areas) reporting to a Deputy Director (DD). Each senior manager should be considered an expert in their areas of responsibility. The DD is chosen by the new politically appointed Top Executive (TE) from within the organization based on one's success in managing two or more of the six areas. The TE can choose their own DD but only from among their senior managers.

- All top field managers would report to the Deputy Director. The field manager has two operational and one administrative managers; all field employees report to them. The DD manages the top field managers with the support of HQ managers as needed and reports to the Top Executive. There are no regions or regional staff. The Director has one administrative staff that supports all senior managers; there is no other staff support of any type provided senior managers.

- The six senior managers at HQ should have no more than the equivalent of 3 GS-15 managers, and each GS-15 manager with at least 24 employees can have two GS-14 team leaders. To be eligible for team leader, a candidate must have successfully served a minimum of three years at GS-13 and two years at GS-12 levels. There are no "special assistant" support staff for GS-14, GS-15 or senior manager levels.

- All organizations under 4,000 employees would be consolidated with other smaller organizations eliminating duplicative administrative staffs. At a minimum, pay, personnel, procurement, and travel should be automated and centralized throughout government.

Management and Planning Staff (MPS)

Each large government organization needs not six or seven staffs as is typical but one relatively small central staff, call it the Management and Planning Staff (MPS). The MPS is headed by a career SES that reports directly to the top executive of the organization *and* to OMB. The MPS staff examines the organizational climate and performance and oversees organizational plans and budget, change and redesign. Its primary mission is to ensure through its independent review capacity that what needs to be getting done in the organization is getting done, and that management actions are cost-effective and employee morale and performance is high.

MPS ensures that:

- A healthy amount of constructive and honest feedback continuously flows throughout the organization. Senior management and field managers meet quarterly with employees to discuss problems and issues and address concerns. The top executive also meets with employees in randomly selected units periodically to answer questions as part of an "open door" or "town hall meeting" approach.

- Annual employee surveys are conducted and analyzed to acquire feedback on the organizational morale, relations, sense of achievement, congruence of perception on policy, and overall work climate. Input is received directly from field units on unresolved issues with HQ and program managers and regarding recommended work improvements.

- An annual independent review and report is provided to the Director on the performance of the organization toward meeting its program and internal control standards and its national goals. The report also includes an independent assessment and recommendations regarding the need for any change to the structure, functions, or work processes of the organization and provides feedback on the impact and progress on the past year's change efforts implemented by the top executive.

- A "Best Practices Program" and "Employee Suggestions Program" promote and reward good ideas that have been successfully implemented within an organizational unit or might have potential for improvement. The MPS also provides follow-up support in the tracking of policy issues, special studies and projects, initiated by the Top Executive, providing feedback on the meeting of timelines and resolutions.

The MPS is in charge of budget formulation, and resource allocation and execution. The MPS also administers a decision support system that provides the top executive and senior managers with timely information on workload, accomplishment, productivity, and program and Performance Plan progress overall and by unit. The PMP ensures that the organizational structure and management is working effectively to get the most productivity possible from existing resources.

MPS coordinates the development of Performance Plans, and tracks significant corrective actions planned and completed by all units. Based on productivity results and the Performance Plan accomplishments, MP provides staffing and resource allocation recommendations to the top executive for all organizational units and tracks expenditures. The allocations are provided one time per year, approximately one month after the appropriation is passed.

MPS coordinates policy, program, resource and performance issues with the appropriate program managers and organizational units, ensures that they are provided feedback, encouragement, support, and guidance. MPS also promotes employee feedback and input, keeps the top executive informed so managers are accountable for meeting goals that they helped to set, and seeks to make every unit a place where all employees enjoy to work. It keeps track of significant initiatives and promotes ideas that might produce organization-wide improvements. Although not all improvements can be replicated by all, tracking improvement efforts can prove invaluable toward promoting positive change, as the best ideas become the benchmarks for all districts. MPS reviews ideas implemented that resulted in improvement or cost savings either in the administrative and operational areas. These are acknowledged in the budget process to indicate what the organization is doing to improve and become more cost-effective. The staff identifies how these savings offset the need for additional resources.

Performance Management Program

Once government Headquarters units and management and oversight staffs are under a minimum structure and uniform design, the next step is to implement a government-wide Performance Management Program (PMP). This program integrates the spirit of most Governmental reform mandates including FMFIA/A-123 (internal controls) and the GPRA (Government Performance and Results Act) into a single cohesive management structure. The PMP links management assessment, planning, budgeting, program review activities, communications, supplier/customer services, and program operations with performance operations.

The PMP consists of assessing operations and activities; correcting actions and plans and implementing improvements to performance; and also tracking the planned and actual improvement efforts. The program calls for a Performance Plan from every organizational unit (e.g., headed by a GS-14 manager in the Federal government) that includes a self-assessment and a manager assurance (e.g., by the GS-15 manager) that acceptable internal control standards and performance objectives are being met and the organization is moving toward meeting optimal levels of performance.

The PMP involves:

- tracking three significant cost-effectiveness and outcome measures;

- meeting seven significant plans and goals within the current budget that would make a real contribution to the improvement of the organization; and

- meeting the ten most important program and internal control performance standards.

Additionally, the PMP calls for the annual monitoring of impact of all funding enhancements; requires feedback from suppliers and customers to ensure that services are meeting expectations; and feedback from producers or service delivery agents on the support of Headquarters. Organizational units are also asked to produce a six month summary of their successes and planned accomplishments and any ideas that can be transferred to other units regarding improved business practices and workflow processes.

Management Council

A Management Council (MC) is organized to facilitate the decision making process within the organization on issues of planning, budgeting, resources allocation, training, policy, and program performance. The Council should provide an independent perspective for consideration by MPS and top management on major management and budget decisions. The group should consist of seven highly experienced, intelligent, and proved leaders: two field managers, two operational field supervisors, and three administrative field specialists. The group is lead by the MPS manager and is designed to provide an independent perspective from the field units regarding organizational improvement.

The field staff would serve for two years, and be reflective of employee diversity. The Council would meet quarterly for three/four days in October, January, April, and July. These meeting dates correspond with the PMP report schedule and the timing of major budget decisions that must be made during the year.

The Council:

- Provides input and reviews the Strategic Plan and Performance Plans of the organization;
- Reviews mid-year and end-of-year Performance Plan accomplishments.
- Reviews the Budget Formulation and Execution Plans;
- Reviews the Resource Allocation Plan (positions

and resources to each unit);
- Reviews recommendations on policy, management, programs and audit findings;
- Reviews management performance data; and
- Makes recommendations in all areas in need of improvement, and on management personnel rewards, ratings, and Unit awards.

With senior managers, the Management Council serves as the primary input to MPS.

Headquarters Senior Managers and Field Unit Managers

The role of assessing performance, improving it, and tracking it for continuous advancement is the role of every unit manager in the organization. The monthly workload, accomplishment, and time utilization data reports will be used to determine how productive field units are and how well they are meeting their goals. The PMP process will promote a continuous improvement emphasis within their units. Each organizational component will need to plan and organize their management processes according to the following:

- Prepare input to all plans and planning processes for the Strategic Plan (each January), the development of the Performance Plan (each October), the review of compliance to program and internal control performance standards (each September), and the results of planned improvements (each April and October).

- Perform annual self-assessment by reviewing program/field unit situation and assessing problems and issues with staff. This self-assessment on performance is conducted by comparing unit performance against the past quarter and year, the national average for comparable sized units, and by reviewing and determining if there is full compliance with policies, procedures, and performance across all areas of responsibility.

- Prepare Performance Plan using the information from self-assessment to generate what corrective actions and plans are needed and are able to be accomplished within the current budget spending plan. The Performance Plan Report includes the setting of tangible goals, as well as methods and actions planned for the current fiscal year, and identifying the performance measures that will be used to assess goal achievement.

- Each organizational unit holds quarterly meetings with employees to discuss progress toward meeting performance plan goals; supplier/customer concerns, budget and human resource management issues, and, solicits ideas on ways to remedy problems and improve processes and program operations.

These meetings enable management to address all of the current management, budget, and administrative mandates in an integrated manner. These meetings provide the means for continuous program improvement facilitating planning and human resource management decision-making.

Program Evaluation

The MPS has a component that conducts program evaluations and unit resource control reviews. The purpose of program evaluations is to focus attention on each program by functional area in order to identify types of organizational improvements needed and corrective action alternatives available. The studies are designed to identify policy, program, procedure, and organizational design areas needing improvement especially those that have a potential to promote extensive streamlining and generate significantly improved cost-effective operations. Each review involves management at Headquarters and a sample of field units differing by size (e.g., small, medium, and large).

The unit resource control reviews includes an examination of internal control issues, the utilization of staff, and matters of fiscal control. The review of the unit's use of staff and resources to meet program and internal control performance standards are compared against other like-sized units, the cost-effectiveness of operations, the ratio of management/staff and operational/administrative staff, sick leave and attrition, and staff morale. Customers and suppliers are interviewed. Problems in performance are identified (effectiveness, efficiency, cost-effectiveness, and timeliness).

Each study produces a summary of major management issues and corresponding recommendations for improvement. Rather than simply checking whether there is compliance with policy, the study emphasizes what needs to be done and how it needs to be done. Each review has two project leaders who are involved in all aspects of the review, report writing, and oral presentations. They present their findings and recommendations to the Management Council, and after the approval of the Director, MPS oversees the implementation of improvements.

Resource and Performance Management Schedule

A calendar of events is provided below detailing a brief sketch of the PMP schedule of activities and incorporates the schedule and agenda of the Management Council (highlighted in italics). It is designed to coordinate time-critical deadlines for the PMP, program review, the budget cycle, and the Management Council meetings. The schedule of activities could be as follows:

September 15th Status Report on Accomplishments, Plans and Staffing and Workplan Requests: All program managers and units report on past fiscal year accomplishments as compared against plans, outcome measures, and performance standards, and submits plans for next year. Requests are made for new staff and resources for next fiscal year (beginning on October 1).

MP consolidates information and prepares management report for Council meeting and includes a statistical model (multiple-regression) or work measurement model for the purpose of conducting resource allocations.

October 15th Council Meeting: The Council reviews Performance Plans and budget request as well as the success in meeting previous year plans, program performance and internal controls standards, and need based on statistical analyses. The Council reviews the overall budget strategy and alternatives for the current year. Workload, time utilization, and productivity trends are reviewed and staffing and budget recommendations are made for each program and organizational unit. Recommendations are provided to the top executive on final plans, staff, and budgets for all programs and units.

November 15th Staffing and Resource Allocations: The top executive releases the staffing and resource allocations to each program and organizational unit.

January 15th Council Meeting: The Council makes recommendations on program and unit manager evaluations, and on "best program and best unit (small, medium, and large)-of-the-year" and other available awards based on performance, progress, and initiative demonstrated over the previous fiscal year. Also, adjustments to the strategic plan are developed and a budget formulation strategy (two years outward) is proposed based on this plan, the current and potential environmental impacts identified, and major themes being promoted by the existing Administration.

March 30th Status Report on Accomplishments: The programs and units provide a mid-year report on Performance Plan accomplishments, about customer or supplier feedback and concerns, proposed policy or resource changes, and work process improvement results.

April 15th Council Meeting: Mid-year Performance Plan accomplishments are reviewed and select feedback is given to the programs and organizational units. Final budget formulation plans for the Department's Spring Call are reviewed and provided to the top executive.

June 15th Performance Plan Feedback Call: Ideas are submitted by programs and units on how to improve both performance and the planning process. Specific changes are proposed regarding the PMP program and internal controls performance standards. Best Business Practices and Employee Suggestions are submitted.

July 15th Council Meeting: The Council reviews performance planning ideas and discusses ways to improve organizational performance and the planning process. The Council makes recommendations to the top executive on what performance standards should be implemented nationwide and what changes are necessary to the planning process.

OMB is Reinvented

OMB needs to be restructured whereby it integrates its

management and budget functions, and in doing so, its management increases and budget emphasis decreases. Its main purpose should be to oversee the MPS operations throughout government and ensuring the MPS cost cutting measures and basic performance enhancement operations are working. OMB would only produce a summary budget request to Congress every two years. Aggregate performance, budget and accounting activity would be available anytime directly from the Departmental databases and the government web. OMB's focus is on reducing budget expenditures (e.g., by a minimum of 2% per year per organization) through improved government management. Congressional increases, if any, are tracked even more rigorously by organizations. Financial Statements and private sector accounting procedures are eliminated in favor of a simplified budget execution accounting format that accomplishes the same purpose at a small fraction of the cost, and is automated.

Throughout government, OMB oversees all MPSs and has access to all Management Councils. As such, OMB is kept informed of progress made throughout the year. OMB establishes a fund to reward managers of programs and staff, organizational units in the field, or entire organizations for the improvements made in cost-effectiveness and savings. OMB has its own Management Council made of informed and experienced retired federal employees who review justification for rewards made by OMB examiners and make recommendations to Director, OMB.

OMB must take the lead in the use of the Internet to govern. The creation of electronic networks has not changed the way most organizations do business. The flow of upward communication comes mainly through the formal chain of command and senior officials stay isolated and insulated from the best ideas in the organization. In spite of the Internet and intranets, communication for improving organizations has advanced very slowly. The ability to communicate within and between organizations in government will only improve through efforts to reinvent the basic way it is managed.

As a result of the Internet, and the failure of previous reform efforts, the government oversight structures need to be restructured to ensure that organizations communicate better and government mandates are implemented consistently and effectively. The restructuring will ensure that management improvement and service prevails, budget increases would only be given organizations that have the new standardized management structure and performance processes in place; with highest priority given to organizations meeting GPRA, performance outcome measurement, and tracking requirements. Funding emphasis would then be given to managers implementing new initiatives to improve work processes and results and/or given to managers having "proven" successes benefitting the customer or contributing significantly to the organization.

Other primary duties of OMB would be to:

- Track management to staff ratios, and operational to administrative ratios, to attain optimal cost effectiveness.

- Implement basic organizational structure improvements reducing in half the span of control and chain of command, and eliminating regional offices and field sub-offices. Eliminate ancillary professional support staff, such as special assistants and others by different titles.

- Improve service and performance. The top executive should only need to go three hierarchical levels (excluding the Deputy Director) down to speak directly with the service provider or product producer.

- Ensure that each government organization has a consistently structured and proportionally sized management oversight staff (MPS) to facilitate OMB policy oversight and administration, and increase government responsiveness to the public and to its own overall cost-effectiveness.

- Assure that each MPS has budget oversight authority for management planning and performance including organizational planning, staffing/resource allocation, performance monitoring, policy and program evaluation and review.

- Reduce government spending by vastly reducing and establishing a uniform management structure and operational process throughout government, requiring OMB's role to shift from budget administration to management of the budget, helping organizations cut costs by at least 2 percent annually, and reduce management structures that will save 50 to 75% of management costs.

Chapter 10

Functions: Ensuring Success of Critical Operations

For big business or government organizations to be successful, certain basic administrative support areas need to work effectively. This chapter highlights a summary of the top ten insights, concerns, issues, or common pitfalls to avoid, in the following critical functional areas:

1. Resource Allocation;
2. Budget Formulation;
3. Policy and Records Management;
4. Planning;
5. Evaluation;
6. Information Technology;
7. Information Management;
8. Human Resource Management;
9. Internal Investigations; and
10. Administrative Services.

Resource Allocation

The primary goal in resource allocation is to distribute the organization's limited resources in a manner that will ensure all employees have nearly equal workload demands and all organizational units are able to meet supply and service requests. While allocations are ideally made on the basis of impartial and objective data, there are many potential subjective factors that can often influence decisions. Based on the fact that resource allocation is often the most difficult and important decision made in an organization, it is important to do it right. The following are some considerations in the process of conducting allocations of staff and resources.

1. The View from the Top

Knowing that the ultimate decision is made by the Top Executive and that this individual has been lobbied or has pre-conceived notions that may affect the outcome of the allocation, it is essential that the top manager be provided all the information needed to make the proper decisions. There are often tendencies to make the most important decisions in the least objective manner. Take for example the following:

- *The Squeaky Wheel Gets the Grease:* Not so infrequently, organizations allocate resources on the "squeaky wheel" principle: "whoever shouts the loudest gets the most." This eventually leads to organizational chaos.

- *It's Who You Know in the Organization:* Often it is not how much the resources are needed, but what support one gets from higher authorities with significant pull that counts the most.

- *It's What Politicians You Know:* Who you know outside the organization is sometimes a most important consideration particularly if the field manager making the request happens to know an influential politician that oversees the organization's budget.

2. Getting the "Rest of the Story"

After the objective data is considered, additional input may be needed to understand better the unique operating conditions and exceptional issues confronting program offices and field units. This might involve the inclusion of input from appropriate Headquarters program and oversight staffs as well as the auditors of field units. It also might include input directly from all unit managers about staffing needs or from a select number of unit managers that would represent the larger body of like-units (ie., large, medium, small sized field units).

While staffing and resource allocations are the decision of the top executive, most senior staff would like to have a voice in the process. Their feedback serves as input that must be weighed against other factors, and typically results in only minor shifts in the allocation results, yet may be very important toward gaining their commitment to the allocation process.

There can be problems, however, if these managers feel compelled to raise matters that they know apply to isolated areas but are uninformed as to their universal application. Aside from unfounded generalizations, the most dangerous tendency is for a senior manager to feel obligated to speak on behalf of someone they personally know, a particular field manager. Here, the top executive must reserve judgment until after checking the details out later from those who prepared the staff work or who may know if such matters have already been considered. If not factored in, it is important not to rush to a conclusion for a single unit. Consideration should be given to whether it is right to honor it for the few without finding out if the issue applies more broadly to the rest of the organizational units.

3. Try not to be too Conservative or Liberal

- *Finger in the Dike:* Too conservative an approach holds back positions and funds and puts them in a reserve and allocates them as problems occur, as a stopgap measure to temporarily plug the hole. The problem is not seeing the massive problem that may be coming soon as a result of not addressing it when able to.

- *Let's Be Fair:* Too liberal an approach buys the assumption that everyone needs resources, so therefore it is only fair to give every unit a minimum number of new positions or amount of added funds. This approach attempts to make everyone happy but it only leads to a growing disparity between the "haves and the have nots" because the truly needy never got the needed level of resources deserved when funds were available and it is difficult to take them from other units later.

4. Allocate Staff and Other Funding in an Integrated Manner

Staffing and resource allocations must consider whether to be provided in an integrated or separated manner. Ideally, it should be a single product including all staff and resources in one package. A budget that is distributed one appropriation at a time, with different types of staff at different decision points, or staff distributed separately from resources, is disjointed. Under such circumstances, it is obvious that the Headquarters components are not focusing on the needs of the unit manager. Also, when budgets are pieced together over time by local administrators, many unnecessary budget execution problems can be created.

Arriving at a coherent end-product for the unit manager begins with an integrated approach at the Headquarters level. It requires that prior consideration be given to the proper size of the uncontrollable budget, the necessity for equipment, travel, and other staff support items, and how much should be reserved for unexpected costs. In this process, it is also important to analyze all assumptions related to "uncontrollable" expenses (e.g., space, telephone, and data communications costs), which may be very controllable and where great cost savings can be realized as a result of more detailed program analysis, disciplined administration, and control of spending.

Another dimension to the allocation of workforce is to ensure that all types of personnel/resources are considered when approaching the task of dividing up the organizational pie. For example, in any government organization, there might be full time permanent staff, part time temporary and permanent staff, and contract staff covering a variety of operational and administrative areas and personnel series. These various types of staff might be funded separately under different appropriations. While the staffing analysis is being reviewed, it is critical that the complete office personnel picture is in full view (e.g., in spreadsheet format) for each organizational unit under examination. Both staffing and resources needs to be considered together for the full picture and both allocated based on workload demands and a realistic picture of true needs.

5. *Try not to be Omniscient or Simplistic*

- *Know-it-all:* This approach may be taken by the experienced top manager who is used to allocating resources on the basis of first hand, personal knowledge of the operations, personnel, and perceived needs of the organizational units. The larger and more complex the organization, however, some form of serious objective analysis are needed.

- *Rule-of-Thumb:* This approach utilizes one or just a few major indicators of demand to justify and allocate resources. The rule of thumb is some measure that has weathered the test of time and generally remained a reliable indicator of need. This approach will not be sufficient in a complex organization.

6. *Allocation of Positions not based entirely upon Appropriated Number*

Determining how many positions an organization can afford to allocate is based on a reasonable estimate of all other possible expenses that may be imposed or come unexpectedly throughout the year. The Budget Chief must be able to assess the projected adjustments to the base budget, such as annual inflation of fixed costs, the hiring and attrition rate of employees, a pay raise, and the cost of salary adjustments. Then, it should be determined if any positions were "earmarked" by higher authorities (the Department, OMB, or Congress) to be allocated in a certain manner, eliminating any flexibility with these positions.

Following a determination of the amount of funds that need to be reserved for special unexpected costs, the remaining amount is available for program initiatives and staffing allocation. The decision between new equipment and new personnel is based on priorities and potential benefits to the organization in meeting goals. Once the bottom line is decided on how much is needed for one-time discretionary use or initiatives, the remainder establishes the amount of funds to be used for staffing. The decision on the level of staffing must be firm because it is time sensitive and must factor in recruitment, testing, and training, and the urgency of immediate staff needed.

7. Pick a Strategy or Combination of Strategies and Refine it

There are three basic objective methods used to allocate resources:

- *Percent Share:* This method adds up the workload in all organizational units and divides them by the total amount of work for the entire organization. The percent of total is applied against the total resource availability to determine allocation level.

- *Performance Standards:* Time-and-motion studies measure work by determining the average time necessary to complete all work activity to meet acceptable work standards, incorporating standards for health and safety and efficiencies for economy of scale. Based on the amount and type of work, calculation of staff/resource need is made for the unit. If the available resources are less than the total need, organizational units receive equal proportions of available funds toward the meeting of their total need (e.g., all units might receive 85% of their total need as the organization can only afford 85% of its total need).

- *Multiple Regression:* Multiple regression models allocate staffing based on workload demands. The results are based on a regression line and equation that depicts a composite average workforce need based on a sliding scale of workload demands. Managers who receive the most work and are most productive each year are given the resources they need for the subsequent year. This occurs because the predicted need is based on workload and performance relative to other units of comparable size.

8. Reductions or Redistributions

Should organizational unit staff allocations and budgets be reduced, or should a major redistribution of existing staff be considered during this allocation cycle? The answer to this question is perhaps the most difficult decision for the top manager throughout the allocation process. The manager must decide whether to cut some units, all units, or no units. It is not the allocation of additional resources appropriated that is difficult, it is the decision to redistribute existing resources the proper way to attain a more equitable mix of workload or greater cost-effectiveness. A revamping of the existing distribution of resources is the toughest choice and generates other issues, such as whether targeted reductions are taken through attrition, the slow way, or, through costly but immediate moves of personnel.

9. One-Time Allocation and Appeal

A fair and well run allocation process is one of the most important elements for maintaining organizational control, productivity, and morale. A bad allocation process has the reverse effect. Although allocations involve the coordination of many parts, much time, and staff effort, failure to do it right the first time often leads to ongoing conflict and continuous problems throughout the year, involving much greater consumption of time and effort.

The allocation process should be coordinated by a single person (or staff) that is in the best position to conduct a non-partial review and has the ability to assimilate all available data and qualitative information needed for successful analysis. The results of a successful allocation and appeals process not only has many tangible benefits for the organization, in terms of productivity and morale, but it has the added benefit of not needing to deal with allocation issues but once a year, except for exceptional and unexpected circumstances. A good resource allocation prevents operational problems and facilitates the budget execution process.

The next question the top executive must consider is whether there should be an appeal process following the allocation. The greater the extent of input from the field units in staffing recommendations and the greater the allocated amounts, the less there is a need to have an appeal process. Field unit managers given a chance to request resources and given a response regarding their request, even if it does not translate into more resources, will not be as inclined to appeal as those who have been excluded from the entire process.

Although largely symbolic, allowing managers a chance to appeal gives them an opportunity to provide expression of their unit's needs on behalf of their employees and in so doing, the manager gains a little more respect from their staff, even though they know their appeal is not likely to be honored.

An appeal process can be handled by memo, FAX, e-mail, phone or in person, if local. In the interest of conserving funds, it should not be allowed to extend beyond a few days or one week, and should not include the cost of long distance travel for those who will wish to make such special appeals in person. The advantage of appeals is that it keeps communication open and lets people vent concerns that they may truly need to express. More importantly, it provides another vehicle to assess real needs that may have been overlooked by all other means of review. Most noteworthy, an appeal can alert Headquarters of special needs that may have become critical only over the last several weeks and was not able to be incorporated into the final analyses.

10. Putting it into a Performance Package

Resource allocations must be viewed in both the context of the moment as well as the future with always an eye on impacting positive organizational performance improvement. Toward this objective, the decision maker must ensure that resource allocations:

- Are tied to the original Congressional directive, purpose, or intent.
- Help organizations pursue their stated strategic goals and performance plans.

- Reflect organizational unit workload, accomplishment, and productivity trends.
- Indicate need based on critical performance factors involving staffing and resources.
- Make prior use of management peer review to assess performance and resource need.
- Take into account compliance with performance standards before giving out additional resources.
- Be used by management in such a way to improve processes within existing resources.
- Consider the use of contract staff for more cost-effective use of resources.
- Compare ratios of administrative to operational personnel, and supervisory to non-supervisory staff.
- Resources are withheld until a plan is approved for their use that improves productivity.

In the implementation of staffing and resource allocations, the top executive must make decisions that will ultimately impact performance. These decisions include what type of the objective format should serve as an allocation foundation; what should be the final resource allocation level for staffing and resources; what complementary subjective factors should be allowed or what type of review and oversight Committee is needed; what type of senior program staff input should be included; what final and integrated resource allocations should be made and whether they will include reductions; and, if there will be an appeal process, how it should be conducted and what staffing and resources will be put into reserve pending such appeals.

Budget Formulation

Aside from budget supplemental requests typically from new legislation, every Department in the Federal Government gets one major chance a year to make their pitch for more resources before OMB and Congress. The length of the agency and organization wish list and number of ways to justify requested resources are almost limitless. This presents a difficult challenge for the Cabinet and organizational Heads. The budget environment is competitive, with budget examiners needing less justification to deny requests as resources become increasingly scarce. This creates the need for more exacting deliberation and science to be injected into the budget formulation process.

The challenge is in determining which types of requests and which methods of justification will be most well received by OMB and Congress. There are certain political realities as well. The political environment may preempt any requests from being given legitimate consideration. In addition, political relations between Executive Branch leaders and key Congressional players will also add a subjective element to the decision process.

There are certain budget formulation approaches however, that should guide organizational leadership in developing a strategy for requesting additional resources. The first step necessary is to bring some order to the process of deciding what to request. Budget formulation requests can be classified into three primary areas:

- responding to public issues, concerns and pressures for new initiatives;
- developing more effective program operations (including the need for operational support and administrative staff); and,
- advancing the organizational infrastructure (facilities, space, property, cars, computers, communications, etc.).

Organizing budget formulation strategies under these three broad categories will facilitate the next step in the decision making process, the ranking and prioritizing of requests. No organization gets all it wants, so it is a question of what is needed, and more realistically determining what oversight organizations believe is needed. It is important to prioritize organizational needs according to the perceived level of acceptance by Department, OMB, and Congressional staffs.

Organizations can spend too much time or too little time preparing their budget requests, include the lowest level employees in generating ideas or have the involvement of only the executive staff, the senior management staff, or just the Budget Staff. None of this really matters if the process fails to construct priorities that will sell to the Department, OMB, and Congress. Here are some fundamental principles that will facilitate the budget formulation process:

- Government organizations are designed to

perform a service to the public and should expand in operation only according to the demands of the public. The budget formulation ranking process, then, should start with the highest priority to reflect public issues and concerns before addressing one's own internal agenda.

- The organization will be better able to gain support for its programmatic initiatives than its infra-structural requests. Infra-structural needs are viewed as matters that well managed organizations take into account as the organization advances The exception to this reasoning is that computers and telecommunications have advanced so quickly that an organization can often justify a one-time expenditure to catch-up with the current technology. (Cunning yet savvy government organizations have had several one-time increases.) Budget execution managers learn to factor "cost cycling" into the base budgets for cars, information technology, etc., to avoid a large sudden need.

- The whole organization benefits when opportunity knocks. That is, once public pressures are placed on the organization for change, the other program initiatives and infra-structural needs will also have the greatest opportunity to improve as well. When there is any new mission, function or expansion of scope, it is ultimately the organization that controls the implementation. In this regard, the organization moves forward at a pace that supports the needs of the entire organization, not just that part that touches the new portion defined by the environmental pressure. Congress appropriates and controls spending at broad categories of expenditure; organizations control actual expenditures at levels that often make it easy to shift resources according to internal needs.

- The weaker the environmental pressure, the stronger and more empirically based should be the description of needs and justification in order for acceptance of the budget request. The most effective way to gain acceptance of budget requests outside of public pressure is to find ways to create public pressure. One way is to use consultants with a reputation of objectivity to assess organizational needs and then widely report the results. Another approach is to request the involvement of oversight staffs from the Department, OMB, and Congress in the review of organizational activities. Both efforts are attempts to improve the objectivity and statistical support of the budget formulation process and lessen the sense that the budget request is simply a selfish pursuit.

- Meeting new and ambitious program goals are not as important as protecting, securing, and ensuring the proper maintenance of existing organizational operations. That is, before the organization can move forward, it must be careful not to create conditions that would result in internal fraud, waste, and abuse of resources or staff. Thus, in the hierarchy of funding possibilities, it will be easier to justify the need for resources to fix internal control problems than it will be to pursue new goals, as Congress will ask the organization to get its shop in order before giving it for more resources and responsibility.

Based on these principles, the following are ten budget formulation strategies:

1. Immediate or On-going Crisis.

If the public defines a need and the media keeps attention on the subject matter in the newspapers, radio, and TV, then the potential for public funding is the greatest. The budget formulation package would need to make the case on how the given governmental organization could help deter, prevent, or ameliorate the difficult or disastrous situation confronting the public.

2. Uncontrollable Expansion of Mission Functions or Scope

If there has been a unique increase in responsibilities for the organization as a result of new legislation or policy, then there is compelling reason to support additional funding. The budget justification needs to include actual and projected impacts, using the most sophisticated statistical models possible. For example, regression analyses of historical trends of organizational demands and resources might show how projected demands are increasing at levels far exceeding the organizational resources to deal with it. The analysis would provide a cost estimate of what resources would be needed to accomplish the current level of program performance.

3. Recommendations Requested by Oversight Organizations

If recommendations have been made by the General Accounting Office, or by the Department, OMB, or Congressional leadership, these are natural reasons for needing additional funds. The goals, requirements, and recommendations would need to be translated into measurable terms to avoid confusion and ensure that the money will meet the intended mark.

4. Results of Internal Performance Monitoring and Internal Control Assessment

This level of review explores the following three basic questions:

- Are there any financial audits, program reviews, or organizational studies that reflect the deficiency of resources?

- Have there been any internal control objectives unable to be obtained due to the lack of resources that directly or indirectly contribute to fraud, waste, and abuse of organizational resources?

- Is the organization able to maintain an acceptable minimal level of program performance and meet standard operational procedures?

The justification for resources must include a specific rationale as to why such improvements in performance require additional resources instead of simply a shifting of resources from other areas.

5. Response to Meet Externally Set Goals, Objectives, and Targets

Organizational goals set by the Department, OMB, or Congress are often initially perceived in a defensive posture by an organization, as if someone else is trying to control the destiny of the organization. How can someone else outside of the organization know better than the organizational managers themselves? These thoughts are ignoring the basic fact that the same officials that call for the organization reaching higher goals are the same officials that approve budget enhancements to ensure that their goals are met. What better match could there be for successful budget formulation.

6. Respond to Internally Set Goals, Objectives, and Targets

The organization with Strategic (Tactical and Business)

Plans approved by the Department, OMB, and Congress has a much greater chance of receiving funds to support the implementation of these efforts the more the oversight organizations have been involved and are committed to the accomplishment of the plans.

7. *Conform to Independently Established Benchmarks*

The more the organization ties its own performance and staffing to outside benchmarks, the better the chance for acceptance of the need for more resources to achieve the acceptable benchmark. The more prestigious the benchmark and the bench marking organization used, the greater the potential for funding. Some examples of bench marking are the American Correctional Association that establishes minimum acceptable standards for the construction of correctional facilities. Another example was the Grace Commission that established the relative level of staffing needed for certain kinds of administrative work existing in any type of government organization.

A similar effect is realized when a top accounting firm reviews the organization, and based on an objective instrument for comparison with other organizations, is able to attest that the organization is in need of a resource increase. The credibility may not be as great as the examples above, but there is an inherent advantage of the independent source's opinion if there has been consistent and ample use of the method of measurement against other organizations.

In any case, success in finding funding is based on the extent that an organization can empirically state how resources are needed to meet the minimum acceptable levels of performance as established by these types of independent organizations or experts.

8. Creating Staffing Parity among Like Organizations or Organizational Units

Unless managed centrally, staffing allocations often conform to the personality and ambitions of the unit manager. This leads to widespread disparities in the operational-administrative staff ratios and supervisory-non-supervisory ratios. One strategy is to determine what the minimal acceptable staffing ratios should be, and determine how many staff are needed to bring the organization into compliance with this level. Another strategy is to compare the same ratios of comparable organizations to the national ratios found in one's own organization. This is an effective method provided that the ratios are pointing to the need for more resources. This strategy, however, could backfire with the other organizations being reduced based on the same study results. The justification would almost always need to include a statement concerning the impact of staffing disparities on employee morale, turnover, and performance.

9. Organizing the Request by Controllable and Uncontrollable Workload

The three categories of budget areas can now be reduced

into two different areas based on whether the workload is uncontrollable (influenced by outside forces) or controllable (influenced by forces internal to the organization).

Uncontrollable Workload
- Increased positions or workload emanating from front-end input organizations (suppliers);
- New legislation instituting new or increased missions; and,
- New policy or program changes instituted by suppliers.

Controllable Workload
- Self-initiated efforts to expand or upgrading existing operation or support; and
- Self-initiated efforts to improvement programs.

10. Organizing the Budget Presentation

Budget requests can be organized for presentation purposes into the categories of uncontrollable and controllable. The uncontrollable workload only needs to be stated in well-defined factual terms, while the controllable workload must be proved to be cost-effective. Uncontrollable increases will be accepted by authorities more easily than controllable workload requests. This factor should be considered in the ranking of the request.

Policy, Records Management, and Freedom of Information (FOIA)

The ten top considerations here primarily concern the important links between policy, records management and Freedom of Information are:

1. Facilitate policy development through records management

Policy consists of any decisions that affect the manner in which an organization conducts its business. As such, this includes all policy directives and other types of decisions such as how budgets are justified, program plans developed, positions and resources allocated, internal controls assessed, performance monitored, studies and audits conducted, and major decisions made. Depending upon the formality of the organization, there may be many important policy actions that occur without official policy directives. While these policy actions may await written policy articulation, for records management purposes, they are vital records and need to be treated as such.

Any decision that affects policy will alter the course of organizational action, and by nature, are valuable records. At the same time, the ability to maintain detailed records on the development and implementation of policy, and to be able to learn quickly from past mistakes, will affect the future welfare of the organization. Good records management helps to produce good policy because decision makers know that documentation is kept on the important decisions of the organization. This creates the incentive to produce policy that is clearly articulated, well conceived, and fully coordinated where managers can expect to be held accountable for the long term.

2. Inform managers of the importance of records management

Occasionally managers assume new positions without the benefit of prior knowledge and experience in the position and little or no verbal orientation. Without proper records, it will be difficult for such managers to know how decisions were made under what circumstances. Records management is helpful to new managers that ponder the origin, background, and history of management decisions of the past effecting policies and programs that they now are responsible for implementing.

Records management helps managers know why decisions were made to create or change policies and procedures; develop or reorganize staffs; build or dismantle facilities; develop, modify or eliminate programs; purchase costly equipment; establish, renegotiate, or terminate contracts; or procure systems, products, or services. It helps managers know how resources were justified; what plans were prepared to expend appropriations; what productivity was achieved; and, what program outputs and outcomes resulted.

Records management is important for the effective daily

administration of organizations, the basic office management activities that make the difference in an operational unit either being efficient or disorganized. It impacts the development, analysis, and coordination of policy as well as the management, organizational performance, and adaptability of the organization.

3. Build a strong electronic records system

Records management is critically important in the current age of rapid change in organizational structure and technology. As organizations downsize or become reinvented, and as paper documents and files are converted to electronic records and files stored in employee PCs, the effort to preserve records becomes more challenging. Electronic records management can produce cost savings in time spent retrieving vital records, in basic office operational efficiency, and in the reduced need for files and associated space.

4. Use records management to improve organizational accountability

Without strong records management programs, there is little accountability for decision-making. Organization, program, and management performance is essentially not open for review. Decisions that change the structure, functioning, or positioning of programs and personnel are implemented with little documentation, and without records, there is no objective review able to be made at a later time regarding the efficacy, fairness, or cost-benefit outcome of the decisions.

Records management can trace the vital signs of an organization's health. Knowledge of organizational outputs and processes become blurry if proper record keeping is not maintained. For example, detailed records are needed when data definitions are changed, ADP system enhancements introduced, reorganizations implemented, or policies initiated. If there are no records, it will be impossible to assess impact. Sound decision making is dependent upon the quality of the records management program.

5. Use records management to make informed decisions

Records management should be thought of more as a critical management tool, like a pilot's black box, a sailor's journal, an architect's blueprint, or a travel's map. It helps the manager know where the organization has been, what might be needed to stabilize an unsteady operation, and give insight as to where it may need to go. It also provides for policy accountability, which is not inherently easy to administer in the government.

A strong records management program serves as the single point of contact for vital information concerning the organization. Such a staff provides a clearinghouse for storing as well as responding to questions on forms, data or text reports, and correspondence. It provides information on organizational charts, functional responsibility statements, informational directories, and geographical jurisdiction maps. In short, concerning any matter of vital importance to the organization, records management should have the record or know where to go to get it immediately.

6. Interview and acquire records of all employees leaving the organization

Without a quality records management program, when people leave positions, their institutional knowledge goes with them and is lost to the organization forever. Organizational reputation declines whenever its own reputation depends on the vested knowledge of few individuals. Without a strong records management program, for example, when case information is requested from the general public through FOIA or from attorneys regarding civil suits, the retrieval process is not only cumbersome, but is often hopeless.

7. Integrate policy coordination and freedom of information with records management

Several organizational functions are directly related to records management. These activities include policy coordination and analysis; and, other vital organizational records, such as FOIA/PA, the management of forms, data and text reports, and correspondence, and demographic and key document references, such as organizational charts, functional responsibility statements, informational directories, and geographical jurisdiction maps.

With the lack of ease of accounting and tracking government outcomes, it becomes even more important that adequate records are maintained on the decision making process. This includes information on the rationale for the policy choice, and the coordination of perceptions and opinions, pro and con, among peers or other staffs. All of this is vital information for managers in case they might need to make a quick correction of policy actions if policy choices go awry once implemented. Records management, if properly fostered, can help complex government organizations to develop a sense of responsiveness akin to that of competitive organizations in the private sector.

8. Use records to confirm policy debate

Since all policies are vital records, records managers want to produce the best possible polices, and thus are in a position to perform a valuable policy analysis role. At the same time, policy analysts need a firm footing in the history of past policy development in order to review and wisely advise on the proper policy choice. In this respect, they rely on records management.

With a strong records management program, policy and organizational responsiveness improves. Policies are developed with the understanding that they will be previewed for validity and reviewed after implementation for reliability. Acceptable policy, with well documented peer review, must then also withstand the test of field staff scrutiny upon implementation. This process leads to better policy and better, more responsible organizations.

Thus, the linkage of policy analysis to records management is critical to organizational health. It is important both to formalize inarticulate policy actions within the organization and to properly document how important decisions are made within the organization. This includes the rationale, as well as the dissenting opinions and alternative policy actions available but not chosen. The combination of records management and policy analysis/coordination duties within the same authority structure facilitates both individual activities and the organization in a synergistic fashion.

9. Facilitate public feedback through records management

The Freedom of Information Act and the Privacy Act (FOIA/PA) require government organizations to respond in good faith to requests for information from the general public. The effort requires finding the necessary information requested and, determining how much of the information should be released to meet the spirit and intent of these two disclosure statutes.

Records management has an important role to the improvement of FOIA/PA compliance. The better the record keeping business of an organization, the quicker an organization can retrieve the information sought by the public. In many instances, it is the retrieval of information that is the most difficult and time consuming step in responding to FOIA/PA requests.

Also, with a strong records management program, many

FOIA/PA requests could be answered immediately in the negative, since the record is destroyed as required by regulation regarding the length of time that such records should be kept. For example, if a record is known to be disposed of following a five year period, the records management program ensures that it happens and prevents the need for an extensive search of "missing" records. Without an effective records management program, organizations frequently must exert extreme organizational energy tracking down information. This includes the request for all employees to search their records for information, or for teams of employees to do nothing more than to hunt down missing information to respond to FOIA.

When FOIA is integrated into the records management function under the same authority structure, the FOIA activity promotes improvements in records management since FOIA is dependent upon effective records management and helps the organization responds more quickly to FOIA.

10. Organize policy, records management, and FOIA effectively

After integrating policy coordination, records management, and FOIA/PA administration into one staff operation, a Policy and Records Systems (PARS) collateral duty coordinator role within each organizational unit is needed to ensure the orderly organization and disposition of policy and records. The PARS staff would organize training opportunities for all unit coordinators. Each of the twelve

Federal Regional Archives Centers has records storage centers and training available. The PARS and their coordinators should inventory existing records and determine which records are unique to the organization and need to have retention and disposition schedules approved by the Archivist of the United States.

The PARS staff would develop a central records system at Headquarters for all important records, and implement a standard record filing system throughout the organization, and align policy and records systems as closely as possible, preferably according to the major program areas within the organization, according to the organizational structure, and hold each program manager responsible for maintaining policy for their own program area.

Planning

Top ten items to remember in planning:

1. Planning involves the unlocking of the status quo

Planning requires strong support and commitment of the top executive, enough to overcome any pockets of resistance among the senior management levels in the organization. Planning does not happen unless each level of management buys into it because planning hints at accountability. If the President and Vice President do not insist upon it, the cabinet official does not do it. If the Department Head does not insist upon it, the organizational Head does not do it. If the Organizational

Head does not insist upon it, the senior program managers and unit heads do not do it. Every governmental planning effort dies from the lack of commitment from above. Until there is uniform commitment from the top, planning is neither consistent nor organized.

Without direction, the amount of planning pursued in a typical organization eventually becomes little or none.

Planning efforts must have some baseline for performance comparison and thus there is a need to document what is currently being accomplished before launching a planning program. While most organizations have some experience with specific project plans, most organizations fail to plan other than to ask for more resources. GPRA asks organizations to get the most from the resources they currently have, therefore, plans for the current year should be ambitious, completed within the current budget, and independent of budget increases. Plans that include the need for additional resources should be separated from the requirement of managers to plan to do the most with what they have. Managers have been known to do nothing new until they get sufficient resources to do it. Managers should be held accountable and have a vision that includes substantial progress toward increasingly greater goals each year.

2. Plans are vital to organizational progress, but must be done right to succeed.

Planning typically requires three levels of

conceptualization. It starts with broad goals that are then pursued through more specific objectives which are followed by specific tasks. Each sublevel relates to the fulfillment of the level above. The larger the plan and longer it takes to develop, the harder and sooner it falls. Plans need to be precise and performance-driven, not expansive and wordy. Every long drawn out planning exercise ends up with all the other plans that have been too lengthy and untimely. Every government planning process, even going back to the old PPB, MBO, ZBB days, suffered an early death by being overweight, untimely, and inflexible.

Plans need to be organized with priorities clearly stated within program areas and among cross-cutting areas. Planning takes hold when the manager in charge of overall planning is central to the senior management team and fully supported by the Organizational Head, and is given full charge to develop the Plan with full engagement of the senior managers and staffs.

Plans need to be flexible, living documents able to be adjusted quickly and constantly to add new priorities, eliminate plans that are overtaken by events, and elevate or reduce emphasis on other plans. Planning is not an academic exercise. Discussions of whether planning processes are, or should be largely rational, long-range, and logical; or should be incremental, short-range, and disjointed are merely academic. Rational plans can be just as faulty as incremental ones. Large scale plans (large equipment purchases, facility development, or ADP procurements) may appear rational, but in reality may be the result of poor planning efforts, just bureaucratic report writing exercises, and may show no more foresight than incremental plans.

3. The best plans solicit input from all levels and across all sectors of the organization

Many plans fail to get sufficient employees feedback. The seeds for the best plans come from the ground level. Until managers listen carefully to employees from all levels of the organization, they will not be able to formulate plans that meet the true needs of the organization and its employees. Planning does not work well in large groups. Comprehensive plans are best created by a few well informed individuals who in preparation of a draft Plan seek to supplement their own knowledge by getting direct feedback from unit managers close to the action and program experts on their ideas.

Once the plan is drafted or outlined in fairly good detail, it should be introduced to a group selected by the Director and presented as an outline simply designed to stimulate thought and discussion. The group would modify and refine both the program specific and cross cutting plans.

4. A distinction between planning and budget formulation must be made clear to senior managers

Planning drives budgets and budgets affect plans, but budget planning is not the same as organizational planning. When planning is halted, organizational inertia and backsliding occurs. Plans should not stop nor be dependent upon budget requests. Managers who show leadership continue to be creative and improve productivity with existing staff without additional resources. Despite budget outcomes, competitive or smart organizations adjust to meet the requirements imposed by the environment. Budget requests are an incidental byproduct of an organization's planning dynamics. Planning enables leaders to drive the organization forward through continuous improvement. Budget success makes everything easier but should not replace the need for improvement processes. Managers who fail to plan because budgets are not funded will fail to set goals, and lag far behind in making progress toward organizational improvements.

5. *There needs to be GPRA follow-through*

The Government Performance and Results Act require agencies to prepare strategic plans, annual performance plans and measures, and annual performance reports. This same requirement must be made for organizations and it should be made relevant to all organizational units. In the spirit of the Act, organizations should plan and measure effectiveness, efficiency, timeliness, and cost-effectiveness, and implement internal processes that promote assessment, corrective action, as well as tracking and accountability.

6. The focus is on performance outcomes

GPRA requires senior managers to think of their programs in terms of organizational impacts. The objective is to review primary goals in comparison to actual performance using specific measures to determine if organizational purposes are being fulfilled. This requires more than budget tables being reorganized into different formats for budget submissions that reflect nothing new about the organization. Rather, it requires the organization to build an internal engine that promotes planning, accountability, and improvement through continuous assessment, corrective action, and tracking. The engine needs to track program and internal control performance standards and use these to objectively evaluate individual, group, and organizational performance.

7. Planning will be resisted

Planning comes naturally to a leader who understands its purpose and place and uses it wisely. Some of the strongest managers, however, are not leaders, but organizational survivors. They seem to know everything about the organization but all their decisions are based on only further securing or increasing their own power base in order to maintain control over their future destiny. These managers keep the organization moving cautiously. It may not always be moving in the right direction, and may very well be steering off course, sideways, or backwards, but it will always be moving in the best interests of the managers. Weak managers resist planning and accountability and drop planning entirely as quickly as they are able to.

8. Planning needs successful implementation to succeed

The amount of planning does not equate with organizational success and improvement. When a planning staff exists for the purpose of management to feel good that it is planning, planning becomes not much more than an intellectual exercise or is ignored altogether. When planning is done without enthusiasm, this is the first sign that the organization is in trouble. This occurs typically when the planning staff is isolated and not a part of the senior management discourse and decision making. On the converse, when planning is thought to be essential, it is integrated into all organizational programs and levels and planners become mostly assimilators, coordinators, facilitators, and promoters of ideas. When planning is sincere, planners meet much success, the implementation of plans is usually swift and comprehensive, and its effect on organizational achievement is significant.

9. The most important part of the planning process is the assessment and commitment processes

Assessment and commitment is gained by unlocking organizational inertia. Successful planning promotes an analysis and dissemination process whereby assessment results become known vertically and horizontally within the organization and commitment to improvement is quickly crystallized. This means that implementation time frames are shortened and urgent, but this is a problem that most planners live to have.

10. Planning and accountability are interdependent, without one, the other could not be effective

Accountability is not possible without plans and plans are not implemented effectively without accountability and consequences. Some of the primary things that are needed to make plans work are the ability to send updates to plans from the organizational Head quickly via e-mail; the ability to track plans centrally from a database whereby all managers can access and update progress on their own plans on a regular basis and where feedback from the organizational Head is provided along with real rewards and sanctions.

Evaluation

Program evaluation is the assessment of the effects of a government service against its purpose and goals, a measurement of the impacts, both positive and negative, for the purposes of making recommendations for resolving problems and improving program processes and effects. Every program has a mission for which it was intended, but these missions often are forgotten as time moves on and data is not collected on program success. This is when programs typically gain a life of their own, beyond the original intent of Congress or the Administration. Aside from the study of legislative history, the research evaluator must rely on the program manager to discern the program purpose and intended program outcomes.

- What is the short and long range intent of the program?
- How does the program manager know when the program is attaining the results expected?
- What measures or indicators point toward the success of the program?
- What are the possible short and long range dysfunctional effects of the program?
- Who benefits directly by the program?
- Who else is affected by the program indirectly?
- What would happen if the program were eliminated completely?
- Who would complain about the decision to end or greatly diminish the program?
- Who would be glad if the program were ended or greatly diminished?
- Why would people be happy or upset if the program were ended or greatly diminished?

The next issue confronting the research evaluator is organizing the evaluation effort and design. Evaluations are typically most threatening to managers who are not used to objective reviews. Most program evaluations are able to provide an analysis of organizational inputs, processes, and outputs, but fall short of reviewing the positive and negative program effects and outcomes. Two shortcomings of most programs however, are the lack of a priori evaluation before program implementation as well as the lack of long-term follow-up evaluation on the program's effects.

Program evaluation methods consist of the following:

1. A Priori Comparison

The pre/post test comparison of program results whereby the same population is studied before and after full program implementation (see Appendix A for a simple assessment of staff perceptions).

2. Key Indicator Monitoring

The monitoring of key indicators and trends to determine if conditions or effects are improving or worsening is compared to prior years including periods before the establishment of the program (quarterly current results vs. historical trends).

3. Relative Impact Monitoring

The comparison of effects between areas served by program according to the level of service provided, including those not served by program.

4. Experimentally Controlled Assessment

The measurement of program effects through the comparison of randomly selected or pre-assigned matched participants whereby one group receives the program's services and the other does not.

5. Internal Program Evaluation

The detailed evaluation of the relationship among program decisions, actions, and outcomes to determine the cause of positive and negative effects of the program (every one to three years, the review of critical decisions, operations and consequences).

6. Progress Reporting

The status review of annual plans, actions, and effects on meeting objectives set.

7. Performance Benchmarking

The benchmark review is a review of other similar program operations (managing, organizing, and producing) and their comparative effect on service recipients.

8. Performance Compliance

The review of performance compliance compares actual performance against pre-set performance and internal control standards that directly relate to measures of organizational effectiveness.

9. Organizational Structure Compliance

This consists of comparing the organizational configurations with set standards for staffing and organizing (e.g., the ratio of administrative to operational staff; the ratio of supervisory to non-supervisory staff; overall staff to service delivery staff, etc.).

10. Combined Evaluation

Any two or more designs above are used to perform the evaluation of program and organizational effectiveness.

One of the primary issues in conducting evaluations is to ensure that the effects observed are related to the program and not the result of other external forces. Some evaluations can control for these better than others, but none will control for the effects entirely. The amount of control will determine the reliability of the results. This must be weighed against the factors of cost and time consumption for the study. The most precise design at the least cost and time consumption is always the best choice. Due to practical constraints, sometimes the best design however, is a combination of several types of studies that relate to status monitoring as well as effectiveness evaluation.

Information Technology (IT)

The top ten things to remember in the IT area are:

1. *Make the IT official visible*

The IT responsibilities, because of its resource drain and its importance is often the single most important operations support responsibility for the top executive to understand and monitor. Therefore, every effort should be made to include the senior IT official in regular staff meetings of senior officials as much as is appropriate. This is important for several reasons:

- it enables an open airing of concerns on everyone's part, helping senior managers provide input into future IT plans and also hear directly from top management what the ADP priorities will be;

- saves the ADP staff from becoming a target in the middle of management disputes on priorities;

- serves to educate top management on the ADP jargon as well as the purpose, processes, and funding needed to be successful.

- provides the IT staff a fighting chance against outside incursions into what would be best for the organization, including Cabinet staffs imposing their networks and proprietary software systems on organizations without regard for the organization's own better plans to develop a more cost-effective and integrated open systems IT environment.

- helps the IT staff stay in control of ADP matters and avoid the problems that arise when program managers want to develop costly systems on their own that cannot be independently supported; buy computers that may be incompatible with software planned or existing within the organization; or develop their own local network that will be separate from that of the rest of the organization.

2. *Be careful to hire the right IT people for the long term need*

There will need to be the right mix of well trained computer scientists, with specialists in the areas of programming, user support, network communications, and user training. Each specialty area requires a different as technical specialization. It is essential to hire the right mix for the long term need because it is often difficult to move specialists from their interest area into another area of specialization. Keep permanent employees well trained and the organization will be able to continue to improve IT in the most cost-effective manner.

3. *Avoid the IT strikeout that can occur in the use of contractors for development*

A strikeout is when an organization relies wholly on contractors for IT development and service. The strikeout is when the organization relies on them for software development (strike one); fails to provide supervision by a technical expert from within the organization familiar with the software or database language (strike two); and acknowledging to all that the development is so essential that it will pay whatever it must to get the job done (strike three). This combination is deadly and often leads to products that do not meet user needs; are not delivered on-time; and, have tremendous cost overruns, if they even get implemented at all.

4. Avoid the IT strikeout with software maintenance

If an organization is totally dependent upon a contractor for software maintenance and does not have a technical expert in-house to oversee how system development and modifications are being written, but requires that they get done quickly, this will result in another strikeout, with the database code looking like "spaghetti code." Contractors getting paid by the hour or by the number of lines of code, intentionally construct the most inefficient programs. With the logic being convoluted, it makes modifications difficult, costly, and time consuming, often causing unanticipated problems in other parts of the program. Not only will no one within the organization know how the program works but it is likely that only one or two contractors know it, and they can bid up their own salary as a surcharge. Meanwhile, the program operation remains at risk as the organization receives less service and poorer system performance at greater cost.

5. Avoid the IT strikeout with user support

The organization that relies entirely on contracted user support, without technical supervision within the organization, and wants the service to be prompt and to the satisfaction of the customer, is looking for another IT black eye. When contractors work off-site on any type of project, and do frequently for user-support, it is difficult to maintain accountability. Customers complaints go into the contractors, problems get temporary fixes, but real problem resolution will be costly or the response time will suffer. This changes if the contractors work on-site under supervision of a technical user-support person who can answer 99.9% of the questions that are raised and can know when to redirect issues to programmers to make modifications in programs to resolve the user-support issues.

6. Avoid the IT strikeout with regard to hardware repair and maintenance

Again, the combination of total reliance on contractors, no in-house supervision, and the sense of urgency to fix a problem will create an IT strikeout. The contractor has the organization "over-the-barrel" when a contract is written without stringent standards of performance on every type of equipment and repair situation. Most often this is able to be accomplished and the potential strikeout is somewhat easily avoided. Cost and response time are still issues that will become problems, however, unless the contract is closely supervised.

7. Standardize development and purchase of hardware, software, and communication networks within the organization according to open systems standards.

This is an obvious top priority for the IT manager but often the organization does not have the will power to get it done. Some IT managers will seek to maintain an inefficient operation as they can personally benefit by it, as they will need to maintain a larger staff, more supervisors, and it will help them secure or retain a higher salary. Having open systems, rather than proprietary operations, will lead to lower costs and better performance in the long run, and often in the present as well.

8. The IT manager must always do the right thing for the organization.

There are many reasons why an IT manager might opt for self-preservation over doing what is right for the organization. For example, the IT manager may fail to recommend to the top executive the right course of action because there is pressure from the Department to take another more costly and less effective approach that is favorable to the Department. The IT manager may, for example, be promised the support for a larger staff, more resources, an incentive award or even a grade increase, for supporting a Department-sponsored program, instead of what is best for their organization.

The IT manager can easily play the game, sell out the organization, and serve one's own self-promotion because of all the areas in the organization, the Top Executive will typically know very little about IT matters. Decisions designed to enhance one's own position almost always lead to poorer system performance and more government waste. The bottom line is the IT manager must never allow selfish motives, power struggles, Departmental pressures, or fear, to obscure their decision making and personal integrity. Resource expenditures must always be in the taxpayers' best interest.

9. Have the long range plan clearly in mind when hiring IT personnel and establishing the proper mix of contractors needed in all categories of work.

The IT manager should look upon each personnel selection and the determination of contract staff as a vital decision impacting the health and future of the organization. Often IT staffs acquire personnel who have "an interest" or "are good at" computers. These folks may be self-taught dabblers or castaways from another staff, but rarely are they the right selection for the IT staff. Each position that is not filled properly with a well educated and highly talented individual is an opportunity lost.

10. Strive for constant systems enhancements until all systems are integrated and accessible from a single workstation through open systems technology that is easy to upgrade and maintain.

Surprisingly after many years of computers, organizations are still operating with a range of data control and decision support problems. Data entry duplication and error, separate stovepipe software applications, incompatible databases, lack of decision support systems, are just some of the problems that still face many organizations. The IT manager always needs to be simultaneously maintaining what is, and developing toward the ideal.

Information Management

The management of information is often the difference between effective and ineffective decision making and between successful and unsuccessful organizations. Managers of information must:

1. Ensure that performance data is used by senior managers

Information that sits idle is like a car that sits idle, doing nobody any good and costing resources to maintain. Managers need to use performance information to improve operations, for example, by comparing program performance and staffing ratios to determine productivity of programs nationally and locally. Where there are large disparities in workload and accomplishments between comparable sized work units, determine why this is the case, and try to help correct the problem in consultation with the field unit.

2. Design organizational checks to ensure data integrity

The audit staff should have performance information to review prior to their upcoming audits of field units. The auditors can ensure managers maintain data integrity and information resources as they must for any other vital resource to the organization. The auditor can assess the manager's data integrity and provide feedback toward the manager's personnel performance appraisal.

3. Use IT and GPRA to improve data management

Develop and improve database applications so that budget, financial, payroll, personnel, and time utilization systems are integrated into one system that generates standard reports and makes queries easy for analytical and operational purposes. GPRA requires performance measures that are timely and outcome based. Managers need such information to make wise decisions.

4. Develop primary points of contact for data throughout the organization

Points of contact for data need to be established throughout, kept informed on data matters, and serve as trainers and direct support to others within the local unit, including the managers, to help facilitate operations and program performance analyses.

5. Provide sufficient training and auditing of data

Training on data definitions and reporting and checking information to assure the validity and reliability of information is critical to success. This training should be viewed as a vital part of the job and perhaps integrated into basic, refresher, and advanced training courses. Without a concerted effort to support training on the importance of data, training will not occur and data quality will suffer.

6. Continuously strive to improve the usefulness of data

On an annual basis, solicit widespread input and provide feedback across all vertical and horizontal veins of the organization on goals, objectives, performance standards, and internal controls, and ensure that all performance measures and indicators are appropriate for each program area, unit manager, and for the overall organization.

7. Provide program-specific data trend analyses on a quarterly basis

Providing feedback to senior managers is essential toward meeting plans and goals and for improving organizational performance on trends. Quarterly reports are helpful in tracking the essential activities of the organization and for maintaining accountability and correcting actions.

8. Conduct studies of data processes

Improve information exchange by periodically (every two years) studying the information flow within and between the field units and HQ, and recommend changes to improve the timeliness of data transfer. Organize a working group of senior analysts among Headquarters' programs to provide feedback on information management activities and planning. The objective is to improve data integrity matters; promote analysis of data trends and program activities; review new information requirements within the organization; ensure there is no duplication with existing information; and, assure that all data input and reporting is in compliance with information format standards.

9. Maintain positive contact with program managers, customers, and suppliers

Continuously work to improve external and internal relations in order to improve data and organizational productivity. Develop awareness and outreach with customer and supplier organizations to ensure that a systems approach to information collection efforts is taken and the organization is able to respond appropriately to its environment. Develop and continue to improve the user-friendly data interface for analysts and managers. Maintaining high customer satisfaction of internal and external customers and suppliers, as well as senior managers, is vital.

10. Improve data support to resource decision making

Critical to the success of the organization is providing data reports that:

- Monitor and predict projected impact of resource shifts by supplier organizations that will either increase or decrease organizational inputs and outputs;

- Determine the resource need from legislative, policy, or program changes that impact the organization;

- Identify data elements and standards of performance that determine whether the organizational units and the overall organization are meeting acceptable levels;

- Help determine how to allocate (or redistribute) the limited positions and resources available within any organization, such as:

A statistical analysis of workload demand and accomplishment data (using multiple regression) to determine where positions and resources are most needed;

Data needed for the Allocation Committee (selected field unit managers) to determine the current and historical productivity and performance ratios, staffing ratios and compositions, management style and employee morale, results of audits, and special operational problems and conditions.

Summary allocation history and recommended resource level by unit. (The Committee makes its recommendations and the Director makes the final resource allocation decisions based largely on the integrity of the data.)

Human Resource Management

Human resource management needs to stay engaged in the critical decision making in the organization and as such must:

1. Improve the linkage of the Human Resource Management and Budget Staffs

Both staffs need close coordination for the control of expenditures related to full-time equivalent positions (FTE) and the hiring within personnel ceilings of permanent full-time positions on-board. Congress often imposes limited ceilings on both FTE and position levels, if the Cabinet or organizations do not impose their own self-controls. Thus, much coordination is necessary between the two staffs on the speed and volume of hiring and training of new employees by HRM and resource expenditure in salary, benefits, and associated costs by Budget. For overall control of positions and resources, both staffs should assign members to a coordination group to facilitate decisions on staffing and ensure personnel hiring controls are being consistently followed.

2. Remember to factor in budget constraints

After the annual budget appropriation, the allocated number of positions will always need to be set by the budget group, based upon the overall budget condition of the organization. The authorized number of positions and FTE (full time equivalent) may increase as a result of the Appropriation, but the projected FTE "burn rate" of personnel-related expenditures must be compared against overall budget availability and program demands before determining the number of positions to be allocated.

3. Measure staffing completely

The number of positions on-board at the last day of the fiscal year is compared against the Congressional authorized number of positions to determine if an organization has exceeded its authorized limit. This authorized number is not the same as the organization's position control number (PCN) which ties to allocations. An allocation of positions can exceed the authorized position number as long as the effect of attrition reduces the number of on-board positions under the authorized value by year's end. The FTE ceiling requires the total work years to be no higher than the FTE ceiling but on-board positions can exceed the FTE level as much as necessary to reach the average level. Hiring far above the FTE level may signify prior problems in the hiring process (causing a low FTE number) and may cause problems in the future (getting back down to the authorized FTE level). Attempting to maintain organizational equilibrium at the authorized number of on-board (incorporating training, hiring, and attrition) will keep it within a safe range for maximizing budget and staff.

4. Keep staffing terminology clear

Often one finds much confusion within an organization on personnel-related terminology.
The terms that typically need clarification within organizations are: authorized positions, allocated positions, FTE positions, and position control numbers.

The Personnel and Budget staffs must have a common understanding of the definition of these terms and must consistently represent the meaning to all organizational units that depend upon and demand clarity regarding their staffing levels. Every two years, information regarding positions needs to be provided management at all levels so to reduce confusion in discussion of terms.

5. Look to improve process through automation

Human Resources Management must identify workflow process improvements in its primary activities, for example, the flow of the Form SF-52 (Request for Personal Actions) and implement necessary efficiencies. Customer feedback and automation are often missing links in poorly run personnel operations. Automation of personnel matters is needed at the operational, analytical and managerial levels, from the initiation/response on personnel actions, to centralized use of information for analysis and management decision-making. Managers need efficient responses and HQ's needs timely vacancy and personnel data for all levels and all organizational units.

6. Eliminate informal notification of personnel actions

Often when Top Management decides to relocate, promote, or detail someone, the action can be so swift that Personnel office is the last to know. This causes considerable waste of staff effort from backtracking and searching up and down various chains of command for the exact decision point and nature of approval. It also results in embarrassment for Personnel for being the last to know, and can cause back pay problems due to the lack of SF-52 and other information.

7. *Ensure integrity in the hiring process*

All positions must be properly classified, advertised, and competed prior to selection, with all authorizing signatures on the 52 before the effective date. When there is a problem with pay due to the paperwork not being properly prepared, a manager inevitably will find a way to persuade Personnel to accommodate the employee as they should. This process of continuous accommodation enables an organizational culture that requires Personnel to spend an inordinate amount of time fixing problems that could have been avoided.

8. *Keep customers Informed*

There should be periodic guidance on the rules, regulations, and responsibilities on personnel matters, the SF-52 process, and other related issues, such when promotions and transfers are allowed.

9. *Maintain databases*

Data input must be complete, accurate, and up-to-date; so that queries and reports can be easily generated and be valid and reliable. If data is entered at the source, there needs to be built-in system checks to ensure that the data is accurate and unable to be corrupted.

10. Separate arbitrary delays from average counts

There are several types of delays in SF-52 processing, for example, that does not represent the norm but highly inflate the overall statistics regarding the average processing time of SF-52s:

- If a job announcement is frozen, the SF-52 is often put on hold and there can be a delay of months until the action can proceed;
- Often when a position has been approved pending move, the finalization of SF-52 actions may be delayed until "move money" becomes available; and,
- Some SF-52s may be received six months or more before they can be processed or the personnel action can become effective.

Internal Investigations (Inspection Staffs and Inspector General Staffs)

The top ten recommendations involving internal investigations and inspections are:

1. Responsibility for maintaining integrity should rest with Management

Top management needs to delegate more responsibility to managers for maintaining the integrity of the organization. Managers should be responsible for handling less serious cases directly and expediently. Cases that should be delegated to managers or functional supervisors are cases of poor performance as well as minor misconduct and negligence cases involving a single item or incident, where there is no pattern of offense, no significant value financially, or risk of embarrassment to the organization. Employee Relations would decide on the minimum and maximum discipline allowed in the case and record the action taken by the manager. This reduces unnecessary investigative burden on Inspections, empowers managers more appropriately, improves organizational climate, eliminates case backlog, and makes investigations timely.

Some examples of cases that should be delegated to managers for discipline are:

- Tardiness, leave abuse, AWOL, or failure to follow required procedures for leave requests.
- Damage to government property (e.g., vehicles) unless the damage was willful or due to gross negligence.
- Loss of government property of a value less than $500. (Loss of credentials and other minor losses would be met with an automatic discipline, and the case is closed.)
- Minor cases involving careless work, endangering safety, inattention to duty, or negligence in the performance of duties.
- Disrespectful conduct.
- Minor misconduct resulting from failure to follow instructions.
- Misuse of Government franking privileges.
- Unauthorized outside employment.
- Employee Indebtedness.

- Violation of Dress or grooming standards.
- Harassment or conduct unbecoming with other employees in office.

In general, broadly stated definitions lead to widely divergent interpretations of misconduct and enables Inspections to be open to conducting investigations on a full range of minor misconduct. To avoid this, managers ought to be able to attain the facts sufficient to fairly and impartially adjudicate matters of minor misconduct and negligence. This process is mutually beneficial to managers and employees. Management needs the opportunity to correct problems directly to ensure confidence in management and employees need the chance to get their minds back on their work quickly. If there is a question on the nature or disparity of discipline, Employee Relations should serve as consultants, arbitraries, and also monitor the disciplinary practices of management. Inspections should only be contacted when there is serious misconduct, criminal and civil rights violations, violations concerning managers, or investigations involving other districts or outside third parties.

2. Establish a Mandatory Table of Adjudication to standardize disciplinary practices

Discipline standards for adjudicating cases should be detailed enough to distinguish degrees of seriousness within an offense category and factor in the circumstances before and after the incident. Mitigating factors to be considered in addition to the severity of the offense are whether it was a repeat offense, whether the offense had an adverse effect on others, and whether the employee was truthful, remorseful, and forthcoming. The sanctions within each offense category should be within tight limitations to minimize discretion of managers.

Managers should be trained on how to recognize personnel problems and correct them before discipline is required. At the same time, they should be trained on how to deal with problems of personnel requiring immediate corrective action and discipline. Also, as part of training on standards of performance, copies of the discipline policy should be given to all employees with the intent of preventing many of the problems from occurring.

3. Caution should be taken to protect the rights of subjects

To ensure that cases of misconduct will not be opened on employees on the basis of nonspecific, fragmentary or unreliable information, the verbal or written allegation should contain the following three elements: one or more specific allegations; positive identification of a subject employee; and a reliable source (trustworthy and worthy of confidence) for the allegation or complaint. The OI would have the latitude to perform a "special inquiry" on matters not meeting these criteria, if warranted, but no record with the alleged subject's name would be produced, unless the investigation was fruitful.

The name of the subject would be guarded in order to protect the reputations of those falsely accused. For example, under the Freedom of Information Act, a request could be made for any misconduct investigations for a given subject in question. A vague allegation concerning bribery against the subject may have been made by an anonymous caller. If entered into the database under the subject's name, the information for the FOIA request might show the alleged bribery was vindicated by investigation. The individual would still be stigmatized if a news report was released indicating the subject was the "target of an investigation on suspected bribery." Individuals should be protected against this danger by Inspections ensuring that all records are expunged immediately following the investigation of such unfounded allegations.

4. Emphasis must be on producing timely and accurate investigations

Timeliness of the investigation improves the accurate gathering of facts, promotes a greater sense that management is concerned about the matter, and insures a timely response to the complainant, the subject, and the managers involved. It is a critical factor in ensuring fairness to all parties involved in the matters. Also, the sooner the problem is confronted and corrected, the sooner relations, operations, and overall productivity of the unit will improve.

Necessary investigations should strive to begin within 24-48 hours of the allegation. With this approach, the issue can usually be fully investigated within 24-72 hours of case initiation. Following the investigation, the investigators should be able to produce the report within three days and be available at any time following the investigation to provide a verbal report to the Chief Inspector and appropriate senior managers Issue resolution should be no longer than two weeks, in most cases.

5. Establish the position (or collateral duty) of an Ombudsperson

Organizations need an Ombudsperson or Dispute Resolution Person that employees can call to work through problems or difficulties that they may be encountering on the job. Employees often need to feel they can safely talk to someone other than those they work with or for, to discuss problems they are encountering at the workplace. The emphasis of the Ombudsperson. By opening up a new communication channel with the prospect of efficient, non-adversarial resolution of problems and concerns, an organization can expect to significantly reduce the number of complaints and grievances needing to be handled by Employee Relations, EEO, and OI.

6. The role of Inspections needs to be clear

The Inspection staff needs to ensure that the Policy and Procedures manual or directives system is clear, understood, and accessible to all employees, and that all employees are given frequent reminders concerning high risk problem areas. On an annual basis, Inspections should ask all organizational units to inform them immediately of any criminal or serious misconduct and note that all minor misconduct is to be handled by management should be addressed to Inspections any questions, issues, or concerns.

7. Look for ways Inspections can improve the organization

A strong Inspections program helps with the organizations on-going improvement. Inspectors need to inspect all organizational units at a minimum of every three years to ensure compliance with policies and procedures, financial accounting and the internal controls areas of fraud, waste, and abuse. Employees need to be asked questions concerning their morale and the overall office morale; their perception of communication within the office as well as the administration of the office; asked if they are aware of special drug/alcohol counseling programs; if they have any questions or concerns related to training, performance evaluations, special issues regarding duty assignments; and if they have any ideas for improvements.

Each individual would also be asked if they are familiar with personnel policies such as minimum standards of conduct, outside employment, grievance procedures, EEO, etc. They would be asked if they are aware of the occupant emergency plan and policies involving office/document/automation security, ethical standards, sexual harassment, and Internet and phone usage.

8. Coordinate and improve management training

OI, Employee Relations, and EEO need to reduce duplication of effort, clearly define proper discipline for certain actions, and refine roles and responsibilities regarding specific cases and explore ways of making the overall discipline system as fair, equitable, and streamlined as possible. Mid-level management courses can provide training to help managers be able to address those areas of performance and conduct that tend to get individuals in trouble, including tips on how to improve behavior, prevent problems, and meet ones potential and career goals.

9. Automate to reduce unnecessary administrative burden

OI functions much more effectively when investigators are networked with access to a database and where final reports are streamlined. A common database would eliminate a variety of forms and the manual tracking of cases and enable the staff to efficiently produce statistical reports and respond to ad hoc queries. Automation eliminates the need to maintain Investigative Log Books or the case card files and as each inspector sends data on the number of hours expended by case, case productivity can be determined across the staff. This information is critical for showing how long it took to perform different types of investigations and identify where training or process improvement is most needed.

10. Inspector case process issues can be the means to improve staff involvement and commitment

Meetings of inspectors, administrative staff, and management can serve as training purposes as well as a great way to generate ideas for improvement. Questions that often need to be addressed are:

- How does one define case procedures so that investigators know when to stay within the limits of an investigation on a case or when it is right to pursue investigations beyond the original intended case parameters?

- How is one to deal with specific cases in specialized areas?

- When and what type of cases should telephone interviews be allowed and what is the best way to take an affidavit over the phone?

- What is the most beneficial of different interview approaches (styles of confrontation and questioning) and ways of taking an affidavit in person (verbatim versus summary; investigator writes versus interviewee writes own responses, etc.)?

- What is the most appropriate sequence of contacts for conducting a series of interviews in different types of cases (who to interview first and last)?

- How can inspectors improve, standardize, and streamline investigative processes?

Other Administrative Services

Concerns about other administrative services include:

1. Expensive new Federal construction of any type should be heavily scrutinized as Federal downsizing is inevitable given the Federal debt and deficit crises. Government cars should run on natural gas only, used for official duty only, and not used as a perk for employees.

2. A greater percentage of procurement contracts need to be of a fixed price performance basis rather than a cost reimbursement basis. Statements of work need to clearly define requirements in order for competition to be fair and performance outcome to be realized.

3. Financial management systems need to be capable of producing activity-based costing (ABC) reports that help managers understand what decisions and actions are needed. Without ABC reports, the true costs of programs are hidden from scrutiny and it is impossible to evaluate the cost effectiveness of programs and difficult to properly plan and improve programs.

4. Automated property management systems should track property by individual possession. Property that is

shared should be tracked and controlled by the organizational unit. Both need to be quickly assessed annually or whenever the continuity of possession changes.

5. Procurement of small purchases through the use of credit cards should be promoted widely but training and controls first put into place. A clear policy on the penalties for abusing credit cards and enforcement through random and computerized checks are necessary.

6. Solicitation for contract bids should promote new competition, cost savings, and improved performance by allowing companies to come into the work place to assess the conditions of the organization prior to their bid (due diligence). At the same time, contracts with a proven cost-effective track record should be given priority and should be expedited.

7. Financial incentives should be built into contracts to allow vendors to show the government how to realize true savings in operations.

8. Space management needs to work hard at finding the most cost-effective space possible and downsizing the average square foot office space for employees. GSA owned facilities should not be sold at bargain basement prices but should be maintained and improved; high rent space should continually be reduced in the government to reduce costs.

9. Compliance with internal controls needs to be

ensured for all financial operations. Obligations are the amounts of orders placed, contracts awarded, services received and similar transactions during a given period requiring payment. Prior year obligations outstanding should be checked and either validated or de-obligated. Also, there should be sufficient separation of duties to assure that if the same person is obligating and paying for the purchases, then another person is ensuring that the transaction is accurate and authorized.

10. Budget execution responsibilities should not just be an exercise in accountability but must include the ability to track program expenditures and cost-effectiveness of performance.

Bibliography

Bowman, L., Deal T., *Reframing Organizations*. San Francisco: Jossey-Bass, 1997.

Davies, M. and Shellard, E., <u>The Government Accountants Journal:</u> The Value of Performance Measurement in the United Kingdom, Fall-1997.

Drucker, P., *The Effective Executive*. New York: Harper & Row, 1967.

Gibson, J, Ivancevich, J, and Donnelly, J., *Organizations*. Dallas, Texas: Business Publications, 1976.

Hammer, M., and Champy, J., *Reengineering the Corporation*. New York: HarperBusiness, 1993.

Maslow, A., *Motivation and Personality*. New York: Harper, 1954.

Suggested References

Argyris, C., *Integrating the Individual and the Organization*. New York: John Wiley & Sons, 1964.

Bennis, W., and Nanus, B., *The Leaders*. New York: HarperCollins, 1985.

Blau, P., *On the Nature of Organizations*. New

York: John Wiley & Sons, 1974.

Carr, D. K., and others, *Breakpoint: Business Process Redesign*, Arlington, Va.: Coopers & Lybrand, 1992.

Caudle, S., "Government Business Process Reengineering: Agency Survey Results." Washington, D.C.: National Academy of Public Administration, 1994.

Davenport, T. H., *Process Innovation: Reengineering Work Through Information Technology*. Boston: Harvard Business School Press, 1993.

Deming, W. E., *The New Economics for Industry, Government, and Education*. Cambridge, Mass: Massachusetts Institute of Technology, 1994.

Etzioni, A., *Comparative Analysis of Complex Organizations*. Glencoe, Ill.:Free Press, 1961.

Gore, A., *Creating a Government That Works Better and Costs Less*. Washington, D.C.: U.S. Government Printing Office, 1993.

Katz, D., and Kahn, R., *The Social Psychology of Organizations*. New York: John Wiley & Sons, Inc., 1966.

Lawrence, P., and Lorsch, J., *Organization and*

Environment. Boston: Division of Research, Harvard Business School, 1967.

March, J, and Simon, S, *Organizations.* New York: John Wiley & Sons, Inc., 1958.

Meyer, M., *Bureaucratic Structure and Authority.* New York: Harper and Row, 1972.

Naisbitt, J., and Aburdene, P., *Reinventing the Corporation.* New York: Warner Books, 1985.

National Commission on the Public Service, *Leadership for America: Rebuilding the Public Service.* Washington, D.C.: GPO, 1989.

National Performance Review, *Transforming Organizational Structures.* Washington D.C.:GPO, 1993.

Osborne, D., and Gaebler, T., *Reinventing Government.* Reading, Mass.:Addison-Wesley, 1992.

Peters, T. J., and Waterman, R. H., Jr.,. *In Search of Excellence: Lessons from America's Best Run Companies.* New York: HarperCollins, 1982.

Senge, P., *The Fifth Discipline: The Art and Practice of the Learning Organization.* New York: Doubleday/Currency, 1990.

Swiss, J.E., "Adapting Total Quality Management (TQM) to Government." *Public Administration Review*, July-Aug. 1992, 52 (4), 356-361.

Waterman, R.H., Jr., *The Renewal Factor: How the Best Get and Keep the Competitive Edge*. New York: Bantam Books, 1987.

Walton, Mary, *Deming Management at Work*. New York: Putnam Publishing, 1991.

Wilson, J.Q., *Bureaucracy: What Government Agencies Do and Why They Do It*. New York: Basic Books, 1989.

Made in the USA
San Bernardino, CA
27 June 2016